Let's Get It Done!

Let's Get It Done!

Dudley Moore, Jr., M.D.

as told to
Jeanne Smalling Archer

Copyright © 2005 by Dudley Moore, Jr., M.D.

All Rights Reserved. No part of this book may be reproduced, stored in a retrieval system, or transmitted in any form or by any means, electronic, mechanical, photocopying, recording, or otherwise without the prior written permission of Dudley Moore, Jr., M.D. or his assigns.

Let's Get It Done! reflects the opinions, perceptions and memories of Dudley Moore, Jr. The stories and conclusions he expresses within these pages are matters of personal opinion, not necessarily fact, and are in no way intended to be hurtful to any individual or group.

Neither Jeanne S. Archer nor Life Journeys has made any attempt to verify the accuracy of any of the information in this book. The opinions expressed within these pages do not necessarily reflect those of Jeanne S. Archer nor Life Journeys.

ISBN 0-9749148-2-7

Cover design: Alix Christian, Alix Design Ink

Front cover photograph by: Rik Andersen, Office of Communication Services, West Texas A&M University

Produced by:
Jeanne S. Archer
Life Journeys
www.saveyourhistory.com
806/352-6336

With grateful appreciation to my son Gary for encouraging me to put our family history on paper and providing the means to get it done.

Contents

Chapter one	Those Who Came Before	1
Chapter two	My Early Years	17
Chapter three	Crawfordsville, Indiana	28
Chapter four	Moving Around	39
Chapter five	Baylor University	52
Chapter six	Freighters on the Great Lakes	59
Chapter seven	Back to Baylor, Then On to Medical School!	72
Chapter eight	In the Army Now	82
Chapter nine	Early Family Times in Canyon	91
Chapter ten	Our Family Expands	101
Chapter eleven	Practicing Medicine in a Small Town	112
Chapter twelve	A Well-Rounded Life	126
Chapter thirteen	Reflections	139

Preface

After the first edition of my life story, *Let's Get it Done!*, was printed in 2003, many people wanted to read it other than the few family members who got a copy. That was nice, but we didn't have enough books to go around.

In the two years or so since the book came out, physical challenges have made it harder and harder for me to participate in one of my favorite activities, blowing my horn. That meant that the band we started (the Fabulous Five) to raise money for scholarships for the West Texas A&M band probably has played our last notes as a group, which has hurt the fund.

My son Gary suggested that we reprint copies of the book and designate the proceeds for band scholarships. The result you hold in your hands.

Since I was a kid, I've been involved with music in one way or another – either singing in a choir or blowing my beloved bass horn. For the past 15 years or so, I've carried my horn, grunting and groaning into the band hall to practice with students the ages of my grandchildren.

The past couple of years, a very nice maintenance man seemed to be always around, watching me come and go from practice. We'd exchange smiles or pleasantries, and he often looked at me with a quizzical expression on his face. One day, he could hold his curiosity no longer. He said, "Hey, Mister. Are you going to ever graduate?"

I laughed and said, "Yeah, maybe in a few years."

Now that I'm 85 and it's harder for me to trudge into the band hall, I'm getting closer to "graduation," but my wish is to continue to help others enjoy two things which have been very dear to my heart: music and education.

There are so many deserving young people who play musical instruments and want to go to college, but just can't afford it. Even though WT is an inexpensive university compared to many, it's still not cheap. It cost money many kids just don't have.

Scholarship money is the lifeblood for young people whose only barrier to a more successful, promising future is not intelligence nor will, but money for a quality education. If we can do anything to make it easier for them to get that education, then I'm happy.

I want to help as many students as I can because when I was broke and trying to get an college education more than 60 years ago, many people helped me. One of those who helped was a woman named Mrs. Tankersly from Marlin, Texas who donated $10.00 for a scholarship which I won. It wasn't a huge sum, but it meant a lot to me and I've never forgotten Mrs. Tankersly. A little money can make a big difference in someone's education.

We all have to help each other. *Let's Get it Done!*

Let's Get It Done!

Chapter One

Those Who Came Before

Now that I am 85, it's time to put the historical record of our family on paper. By remembering a few of the stories and collecting a lot of photographs, we've done the best we could to compile a suitable portrait of my life so far. If this doesn't do the trick, there are scads of other pictures in closets and desks. My wish is that this book will shed some light on our history and perhaps give some insights about the many people and events which have shaped my life.

My mother was a beautiful woman named Evelyn Mattie Leisk Moore and my father was George Dudley Moore. Weston, my only brother, was two years younger than me. He was born October 13, 1921 in Baraboo, Wisconsin.

So much of a person's personality is influenced by their parents, so before I get too far along with my own story, I'll share a few of the details that I've pieced together about the early lives of my father, my mother and their ancestors.

My Father's Genealogy

My dad born March 7, 1887 in Panola, Alabama which is in Sumter County, just a stone's throw from Mississippi. His mother's name was Susie Weston and his father's name was Thomas Moore, but unfortunately, I never knew them. According to the family stories, Dad and his parents planned on going west, but their house burned down and his mom and dad were killed in the fire. Supposedly, a Presbyterian preacher named Reverend Westir and his wife helped raise my father. They lived in Pasadena, California.

Dad didn't talk very much about his parents, though he did mention covered wagons and going through the country in rain and floods, but he barely mentioned anything else. There was also a story that my dad had relatives in Columbus, Mississippi who lived on a rather large cotton farm in the Tombigbee River area. In the old days, an Aunt Annie lived there and she had 150 mules and 75 slaves. Dad also had relatives who were on a gambling boat when it blew up so the graveyard near Columbus apparently is loaded with Moores.

Grandmother Westir, the woman who raised my father, holding me when I was two months old.

Dad had a brother named Robert, though I don't remember ever seeing him. From time to time, Dad mentioned him but when we went through Dad's papers, we didn't find much information about Robert. Dad had a pretty good amount of land in Alabama and Robert supposedly leased it from him. When Robert couldn't pay him for the lease, Dad lost the land. That was just the way it was. Times were bad and if you can't do it, you can't do it.

Dad went to William Jewell College in Liberty, Missouri which isn't far from Kansas City. It is still a very good, small school. In fact, in September of 2001, *Time Magazine* named William Jewell College the "Liberal Arts College of the Year."

WAR SERVICE

My father was always very proud of his service to his country.

During World War I, he was in one of the horse-drawn field artillery regiments and saw action in France. My dad was involved when the Americans helped France stop the German advance at the Chateau-Thierry, and another time at the Battle of Marne, which was said to be one of the turning points of the war.

One of our country's famous patriotic songs is "When the Caissons Go Marching Along" and it has some descriptive words about the field artillery:

Over hill, over dale
As we hit the dusty trail,
And the Caissons go rolling along...

Then it's hi! hi! hee!
In the field artillery,
Shout out your numbers loud and strong,

For where'er you go,
You will always know
That the Caissons go rolling along.

Dad never gave me many details about the service, but he did mention that his brother, who was a diabetic, was over there at the same time. There was no insulin for dad's brother and he died in my father's arms in a rain-soaked trench. Maybe that was his brother, Robert, or perhaps Dad had another brother. I'm not sure.

My dad, George Dudley Moore.

After he got out of the army as a captain in 1918, Dad and Mom got married. What opposites they were, a Yankee from Milwaukee and a

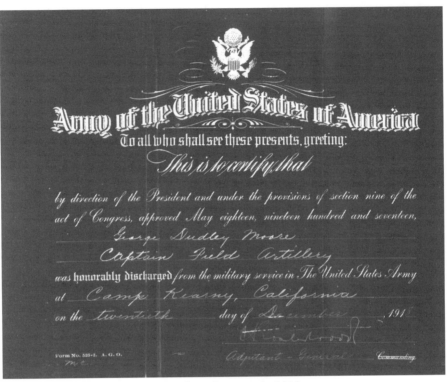

My dad's papers, discharging him from the army in 1918.

> Muscle Shoals Ala
> July 21- 1924
>
> War Dept
>   Wash D.C.
> Subject:
>   Securing copy of honorable discharge certificate.
>
> I am employed on Wilson Dam as Electrician have papers in for foreman In order to get soldiers preference it is necessary for me to secure above at once.
>
> Will you secure same for me or advise how I can secure it speedily
>
> I went to Officers Training Camp @ Oglethorpe Aug 27 – 1917 Commissioned 1st Lt F.A. Dec 1st.
> Attached to 76th F.A. Dec 10
> Assigned to 66 FA Sept 1918
> Discharged Dec 20? 1918
>   George D. Moore   Capt F.A. O.R.C.

My father's letter to the war department.

Southerner from Alabama. They met in a Baptist church in Chicago, got married and started a new life together. What a change it must have been for Mother to go from the Great Lakes — where she had lived all her life — to a coal-mining town in the hills of Alabama. But Mother had her family and she had her church and that's all she ever needed.

Dad stayed in the active reserve for a few years when we were living in Louisville and he trained in Fort Knox for two weeks at a time. Twice, I went with him and I remember getting to ride the old swaybacked horses they used in the field artillery.

BACK TO HIS ROOTS

It is of interest to note a story about the time that my father went with me to a medical meeting in Kansas City, near Liberty, which is where he had gone to college. When I got through with the lectures at the meeting, I suggested to my dad that we go to Liberty and he agreed.

As we got close to the town, Dad said, "Let's go over to the square." When we got there, he said, "We're going to come to a drug store and there ought to be a tall fellow in there working."

My dad hadn't been to that town in 50 years, but it was exactly as he had described. When we got to the drug store, my dad and I got out of the car and walked in. The place was kind of empty and here comes this tall fellow. He said, "Well, Hi, Dudley!" It was the pharmacist that my dad had correctly predicted would be there. For two or three hours, the two of them shared some of the old stories and all of us had a real nice visit. The 50 years that had passed since their last meeting just melted away.

After they talked for awhile, the pharmacist said, "Dudley, they need you out at the college." I couldn't imagine what they needed my dad for since he hadn't written a letter to anyone and nobody knew that Dad was coming. We drove over to the college, and the two of them went into the science department.

I heard a bunch of knocking sounds, which I identified as the sound of hammers hitting a wall. As we walked into the room where the hammering was coming from, Dad's tall friend says to an older gentleman who was working inside, "Here, I found him." It was just like they had been looking for my dad and happened to get lucky that he had shown up!

The man was my Dad's former professor, who at the time of our visit must have been about 90 years old. He said, "George, we're remodeling this room here. Do you remember where we put that water line?"

Dad said, "It's over there."

The old professor said, "That's right, George. You're right! We were looking in the wrong place!"

Dad remembered where they put that line because he worked one summer remodeling the chemistry lab when he was a student. That had been 50 or 60 years earlier but he remembered like it had happened the day before. It was the nicest thing you ever saw.

Dad was always mechanically minded and was very good in chemistry, physics, and electricity. He was an electrician and worked in construction and steel mills a great deal of the time. He moved around a little during his working years, living in places like Pueblo, Colorado and Birmingham, Alabama, where he worked in the steel mills.

When I was born, Dad was working on the Black Warrior River near Gorgas. Later, my dad worked on the Muscle Shoals Dam on the Tennessee River and we lived up in the northwestern part of Alabama around Sheffield and Tuscumbia. Later, he got to be an inspector at Louisville Gas and Electric Company in Louisville. Still later, we moved back and forth between Shreveport, Louisiana and Kilgore, Texas. My early years included some rough times during the Depression and our family just followed the work wherever my dad could find it. I'll get into more detail about that later.

MOTHER AND HER FAMILY

In contrast to what little we know about Dad's family, we know a lot about my mother's side of the family. Mother's maiden name was Evelyn Mattie Leisk and she was born in Milwaukee, Wisconsin on the 4th of May in 1894. I knew many of my relatives on my mother's side very well.

In February of 2001, we learned even more information about this side of the family when a cousin named Harry G. Leisk wrote some family information in a publication called *Sailing the High Seas and the Great Lakes: The Leisk Brothers and Their Ships in the Late 19th and Early 20th Centuries*. It's very interesting and tells a lot about the Leisks. I've got a copy and so does my son, Gary.

The name was spelled Leask at one time and they all came from Shetland, Scotland. On my mother's side, my grandfather's name (according to this cousin) was Thomas Leisk and he was born November 1, 1837 in Houss, East Burra Isle, Scotland. He was the oldest of six children born to George and Ann Leask. Thomas Leisk had three brothers and two sisters and all the brothers sailed on the Great Lakes and around the world. I never knew my grandfather because he died in 1910 about nine years before I was born, but it's really something to read in the book about where they went and what they did.

My mother, Evelyn Mattie Leisk Moore, when she was about thirty years old.

Thomas' first wife, Jane Smith Leisk, died after they had seven children and then he married my grandmother who was Caroline Emma Pitt Leisk. With his second wife, they had five more children:

> Jessie Adeline Leisk
> William Charles Leisk (Uncle Will)
> Myrtle Elizabeth Leisk
> Evelyn Mattie Leisk (my mother)
> Ruth Caroline Leisk

My grandfather, Thomas Leisk.

My grandfather, Thomas Leisk, is on the far left.

My grandmother Leisk was quite a lady, but she hated me. I don't blame her. I deserved it. She was bossy and I didn't want to be bossed. She had favorites and I was not one of them. Hugh Collett, Aunt Ruth's son, and my brother, Weston, were her favorites. Grandma also liked Tom, Uncle's Will's boy, but she didn't think Tom's brother Wardell was so hot. So she had her favorites. That was it. With kids, it didn't make any difference.

She could catch me stealing out of the refrigerator better than anybody in the world. She was blind – presumably – but if I opened the refrigerator, she somehow was always right there looking at me. She was something.

She was a beautiful lady and very stately. With as much poise as she had, she could have been the queen of England and you would have thought that it was just right. Grandmother always dressed very well

My grandmother, Caroline Emma Pitt Leisk, who was born in 1858 in Wales.

and had perfect posture.

Grandma lived many years in Milwaukee. My Uncle Will always took care of her and she went wherever he went. Uncle Will was an oilman in Eldorado, Arkansas who later moved to Shreveport, which is where she was living most of the time when I knew her. Grandma was what I guess you'd call a snowbird. In the summer time – when it got so hot in Shreveport – she went to Buffalo, New York where Aunt Jessie was. Then she'd come back down south when it started to get cold in Buffalo.

She needed somebody to go with her on her travels from one place to another, so it was always my chore to escort her on the train. Everyone took care of my grandmother, one way or another. That's how our family was.

I'd take Grandma with me from Shreveport to Crawfordsville where she'd spend a few days with her daughter, Ruth Collett, then go on up to Buffalo where she stayed with Aunt Jessie. I'll talk more about Aunt Ruth and Uncle George Collett a little later.

Aunt Jessie's husband, Andrew, was a captain on the Great Lakes and they had a beautiful home on Lake Erie.

Just to round out some of the family information on my mother's side, my Aunt Myrtle (Myrtle Leisk Gauss) was married to a professor named Henry Fallenstein Gauss. He worked at the University of Idaho at Moscow, Idaho. About 20 years ago, they built a science building on the campus there and named it after him.

My aunt and uncle, Henry and Myrtle Gauss.

Aunt Myrtle and Uncle Henry had two girls, Mary and Phyllis, as well as two boys, Bill and Joe. The boys were brilliant mathematicians. One later became a vice president for GE in charge of air conditioning, heating, and anything electric which was a pretty good job. The other boy was in the army and taught mathematics and physics at an air base in Albuquerque until he retired.

One thing about it, I have a family that paved their way. They cut a swath. They didn't sit around wanting to be on relief. They were all interested in churches, as well.

Mother only went to school to the eighth grade. Why, I don't know. We recently found an item on the Internet that put her schooling into perspective. An 1895 test from Salina, Kansas lists what those students had to know to pass eighth grade. Perhaps Mother's curriculum wasn't too different. I wonder how many of today's eight graders could pass the same test!

Mother always dressed well, even when she didn't have any money to spend on clothes. When times were tough and she wore the same dress for 10 years, she still looked good. I never saw her that I wasn't satisfied and proud of her. She could sew beautifully and made my summer shirts out of feedsacks.

When Mother and Dad met in Chicago, he was up there doing electrical work and Mother was working in an office. They both sang in the choir. Dad had a beautiful voice. Let's just say that Mother liked to sing.

They got married in 1918 in Pasadena, California. I'm not sure of any of the details about their wedding, but Reverend and Mrs. Westir (who had raised my father after his parents died) lived in Pasadena. I believe Reverend Westir performed the marriage ceremony for my parents.

Maybe, I could say, "The rest is history!"

The following is the eighth grade final exam from 1895 taken in Salina, Kansas. It was taken from the original document on file at the Smoky Valley Genealogical Society and Library in Salina, Kansas and reprinted by the Salina Journal.

8th Grade Final Exam:
Salina, Kansas - 1895

Grammar
(Time, one hour)

1. Give nine rules for the use of Capital Letters.
2. Name the Parts of Speech and define those that have no modifications.
3. Define Verse, Stanza and Paragraph.
4. What are the Principal Parts of a verb? Give Principal Parts of do, lie, lay and run.
5. Define Case, Illustrate each Case.
6. What is Punctuation? Give rules for principal marks of Punctuation.
7-10. Write a composition of about 150 words and show therein that you understand the practical use of the rules of grammar.

Arithmetic
(Time, 1.25 hours)

1. Name and define the Fundamental Rules of Arithmetic.
2. A wagon box is 2 ft. deep, 10 feet long, and 3 ft. wide. How many bushels of wheat will it hold?
3. If a load of wheat weighs 3942 lbs., what is it worth at 50 cts.per bushel, deducting 1050 lbs. for tare?
4. District No. 33 has a valuation of $35,000. What is the necessary levy to carry on a school seven months at $50 per month, and have $104 for incidentals?
5. Find cost of 6720 lbs. coal at $6.00 per ton.

6. Find the interest of $512.60 for 8 months and 18 days at 7 percent.

7. What is the cost of 40 boards 12 inches wide and 16 ft. long at $20 per inch?

8. Find bank discount on $300 for 90 days (no grace) at 10 percent.

9. What is the cost of a square farm at $15 per acre, the distance around which is 640 rods?

10. Write a Bank Check, a Promissory Note, and a Receipt.

U.S. History
(Time, 45 minutes)

1. Give the epochs into which U.S. History is divided.
2. Give an account of the discovery of America by Columbus.
3. Relate the causes and results of the Revolutionary War.
4. Show the territorial growth of the United States.
5. Tell what you can of the history of Kansas.
6. Describe three of the most prominent battles of the Rebellion.
7. Who were the following: Morse, Whitney, Fulton, Bell, Lincoln, Penn, and Howe?
8. Name events connected with the following dates: 1607, 1620, 1800, 1849, and 1865?

Orthography
(Time, one hour)

1. What is meant by the following: Alphabet, phonetic orthography, etymology, syllabication?
2. What are elementary sounds? How classified?
3. What are the following, and give examples of each: Trigraph, sub-vocals, diphthong, cognate letters, linguals?
4. Give four substitutes for caret 'u'.
5. Give two rules for spelling words with final 'e'. Name two exceptions under each rule.
6. Give two uses of silent letters in spelling. Illustrate each.
7. Define the following prefixes and use in connection with a word:

Bi, dis, mis, pre, semi, post, non, inter, mono, super.

8. Mark diacritically and divide into syllables the following, and name the sign that indicates the sound: Card, ball, mercy, sir, odd, cell, rise, blood, fare, last.

9. Use the following correctly in sentences: Cite, site, sight, fane, fain, feign, vane, vain, vein, raze, raise, rays.

10. Write 10 words frequently mispronounced and indicate pronunciation by use of diacritical marks and by syllabication.

Geography
(Time, one hour)

1. What is climate? Upon what does climate depend?
2. How do you account for the extremes of climate in Kansas?
3. Of what use are rivers? Of what use is the ocean?
4. Describe the mountains of N.A.
5. Name and describe the following: Monrovia, Odessa, Denver, Manitoba, Hecla, Yukon, St. Helena, Juan Fernandez, Aspinwall and Orinoco.
6. Name and locate the principal trade centers of the U.S.
7. Name all the republics of Europe and give capital of each.
8. Why is the Atlantic Coast colder than the Pacific in the same latitude?
9. Describe the process by which the water of the ocean returns to the sources of rivers.
10. Describe the movements of the earth. Give inclination of the earth.

CHAPTER TWO

My Early Years

I was born on November 9th, 1919 in Gorgas, Alabama, which isn't too far from Birmingham. It was a coal mining town, and they used the coal to run the generators at the Alabama Power and Light Company.

We moved around quite a bit after I was born. For awhile, we lived in the northwestern part of Alabama, near Sheffield and Tuscumbia.

Me at age nine months.

Mother and Dad with me when I was two months old.

My mother with her two young sons in Sheffield, Alabama.

Weston and me.

Weston and me with our parents in Gorgas, Alabama. I was four and Weston was two.

One of my earliest memories was when we were living in Gorgas. It's a vivid memory, but not a pleasant one. To understand what happened, you have to keep in perspective that we were living in rural Alabama in times much different from what they are today. Different and difficult.

When I was about six or seven years old, I witnessed a Ku Klux Klan meeting. My dad was a member – like I'm sure every other man in town was – and one night he put on this white outfit with a hood on it, and he started out the back door. My eyes must have gotten pretty big and Mom must have seen the look and anticipated what I was thinking. She said, "Now, son, you stay here! You don't go where he's going."

She turned around and went one way, and I went out the door and followed him. When I came upon the scene, I stood and watched this huge commotion from a vantage point about a hundred yards away or so.

There were a bunch of guys in these hooded white sheet-things. Maybe there were only about 100 people, but to me, it seemed like there were about 400 people, all hollering and watching this big cross burning.

I was scared to death. I knew I was somewhere that I shouldn't have been, watching something I shouldn't be seeing. I watched for a moment or two and then turned around and ran home pretty darn fast. Mother never even knew I was gone and I never told anybody what I'd done. It wasn't anyone else's business. I was so scared!

My mother had told me not to go, and I just considered that a good reason to go, but boy I regretted it.

Friends of Color

Even though my dad had been in the Ku Klux Klan, he had at least one very good friend when he was growing up who was black.

Many years ago, I went to visit my parents when they were living in Birmingham. After I was there for a while, Dad asked me to drive him around where he used to hang out. I agreed and we got in the car and drove from Birmingham to Tuscaloosa, then down to Livingston and eventually up to Panola in western Alabama where he used to live.

"Slow down, son," he said when we got close to Panola, "because I want you to turn up here at that rutted road. I want to see if someone is still sitting in a rocking chair outside a house that I remember."

We came up over a little rise, turned the corner, and I swear to God there was the little house with a blind Negro man sitting in a rocking chair on the front porch.

I pulled the car to a stop, not far from the front porch, and Dad stepped out of the car. As Dad walked toward the man, he called him by name. That man recognized his voice and said, "Well, Hi, George." Once we got on the porch, the man and my dad hugged and cried and I did, too. Come to find out, my Dad and this black man had been close friends when my dad was just a tiny little kid. For about an hour, we visited and during that time, the 60 years that they had been apart just melted away. It was something.

Growing up in Louisville

About 1927, when I was about eight years old, my dad got a job working as an inspector at Louisville Gas and Electric. We had a comfortable house on Claire Avenue in a nice part of Louisville called Crescent Hill.

It was a stucco house on a deep lot, about 60 x 40. A few steps led from the sidewalk up to the house. Toward the front of the house was a small room which we used as a reading room or a library. The windows in there were made of small panes of beveled glass which each measured about six inches square. Boy, we broke a lot of those suckers when we played baseball!

It wasn't huge by today's standards, where people need a lot of space with spots dedicated to doughnuts or something. I remember that we paid $45.00/month.

The living room was pretty big. That's where the fireplace was. Somewhere we also had a piano and for a long time, I took piano lessons. We had a nice-sized dining room with the kitchen close by. That's where I spent a lot of time helping my mother. We had one bathroom and two bedrooms so I always had to share a room with my brother.

Boy, we had some great fights, I can tell you! I'll tell the story of a very memorable fight with him a little later.

We had a Model A Ford Roadster that could carry two people in front and two people in the rumble seat in the back. Mother always made sure we dressed well in good clothes, and that often meant white britches which must have been pretty hard for young, active boys to keep clean.

While we were in Louisville, Mother had tuberculosis and was in the sanitarium there for two years. It must have been rough for our family, but I guess the relatives pitched in and took care of Weston and me. Dad hired a woman who took care of us. All I remember about that time is that the woman could make anything out of oatmeal. If we had any left over from breakfast, we had fried oatmeal biscuits at the next meal. I got so sick of oatmeal!

I don't remember that any of us ever went to visit my mother during the time she was in the sanitarium, but I expect that my father probably did. In those days, you stayed as far away from tuberculosis as you could. Kentucky, on the Ohio River, was a prime place for the disease and both my brother and I had Miliary TB— but it's quiet in my lungs now.

Weston, my cousin Hugh and me on our way to Sunday school in our starched, white clothes.

Fun and Games

In our house, the basement was where all the fun was. It was a big room and it was always full of kids playing all kinds of games. I guess we must have all been budding actors and actresses because we'd make up plays and then act them out. It was also a great place to play all kinds of sports. Also down in the basement was a big coal-burning furnace that had a tendency to make things really dirty.

There was an empty lot on the side of the house where we had a makeshift baseball diamond. Unfortunately, that was also the side of the house where the library was with all those little glass windows. If you hit a foul ball – which young boys are prone to do – it would smack into those windows. We had to pay for any glass we broke to the tune of 75¢ each. I spent a lot of money replacing windows!

In the front was a nice-sized maple tree. We'd climb up in the tree and throw rocks at people as they passed by. They couldn't see where the rocks were coming from because we were hidden by the leaves up in the branches of the tree.

Behind the house was a city reservoir with a big hill around it. That's where I learned to ski. We'd get barrel staves and take some rubber off an inner tube, then put them on our feet and scoot down that baby! On the other side was a great big park with a golf course where we played a lot of golf. Sometimes, we'd even devise our own golf course by using a shovel to dig out a hole. We'd even add the roughs. We played all the sports in the world. We were doing something all the time.

When we were growing up, there was a fellow named Alvin "Shipwreck" Kelly who was the acknowledged master of flagpole-sitting, a public fad of the 1920s. As a publicity stunt, he would stand for days on the top of specially-prepared flagpoles all over the United States. At Atlantic City's Steel Pier, he set a world record by perching atop a flagpole for seven weeks. We saw him when he came to Louisville which he did several times. He put a little platform up on the flagpole, and sat on it for hours and hours.

Our version of this stunt was to stand on the top of fenceposts. Seven or eight of us dumb kids would stay all day long on those darn things unless we had to go to the pot. We even devised a very effective system of sending messages to each other as we were standing there. We strung a wire between the fenceposts. If you wanted to say something to another guy, you'd take an umbrella, hook it over the wire, and drop the message into the umbrella. By lifting the wire up and down, you could scoot the message in the umbrella over to the next guy, and on down the line.

You could also use the umbrella to hold other things besides messages, like food. I remember saying, "Hey bud, do you have a candy bar?" and I'd swap something I had for the candy bar. We'd ship things back and forth to each other using the umbrella. It was a handy system and a good way for young guys to harmlessly pass some time. Remember, these were long before the days when people were glued to their television sets.

SPECIAL HOLIDAYS

I don't recall celebrating holidays very much, but I do remember that when we lived in Louisville, we had nice Christmas holidays with a tree and nice gifts. We decorated the tree two or three weeks before Christmas. The decorations were kind of like they are today with glass balls and a lot of tinsel. In fact, when we got it all decorated, the tree leaned with the weight of the stuff we put on. We also had stockings with stuff in the stockings.

It seemed like Weston and I got a train or balls and bats to play with. Electric trains were always my favorite and I always had good footballs and baseballs and tennis rackets. We had a lot of presents and Mother played the piano and sang.

I remember celebrating the fourth of July when Dad took us to Lexington, Kentucky to see the race farms. He had been raised on a farm, so he instilled his love of horses in us. We saw Calumet Farms, and Bradley Farms. We even got to see the great racehorse, Man O' War, who was the daddy of all racehorses – the greatest racehorse that ever lived. He was foaled in 1917 and lived 30 years. During that time, the racing record books were rewritten. He won 20 of his 21 starts, beating the best horses of his time and even winning the Belmont Stakes by 20 lengths. Ah, he was gorgeous.

All the horses of the Bradley Farms started with a B. For instance,

Bubbling Over, Bag and Baggage, and Blue Larkspur. They were all great racehorses. It was about 75 miles from Louisville to Lexington and we'd take all day to see the horses. We'd come back around 9:00 or 10:00 at night. Boy what a day.

Another source of fun was to go to the park and see huge fireworks displays. Towns in those days had nice parks and for the fourth of July, there were always lots of fireworks – so spectacular that you just couldn't believe it. You can imagine, for a little kid, those holidays were pretty special with such magnificent fireworks and incredible bands playing beautiful music.

THE DEPRESSION

One morning while we were living in Louisville, I was helping Mother wash dishes which was what I had to do before I went to school. Dad was in the house, but he didn't go to work that morning. I said, "Mom, how come Dad's not going to work?"

She said, "Well, son, he doesn't have a job."

It was just terrible. I remember my Dad sitting around the house with his head down, just demoralized. One day he was happy because he thought he was going to get to sell a toaster to a family.

Don't let me mince words here. The Depression was just awful, mainly for the effect that it had on my father. Though we were never hungry, Dad lost all his self respect. He was a very academic man and once he didn't have a job, he didn't have any money to do anything. It just wiped him out – just like it would you or me.

I'm sure that Mother and Dad had no savings, but Mother's family must have helped out by sending her some money from time to time. Dad was out of work for four years. I tell you, it ruined my Dad and he had it tough.

After Dad lost his job when the Depression hit, he hitchhiked all over, slept in haystacks and worked whenever he could find a job. For the next few years, my parents and Weston moved all over the south. Among other places, they lived in Eldorado, Arkansas and then in Shreveport,

Louisiana where Dad worked building Barksdale Field which I'll tell more about a little later.

Church Life

From my earliest days, church has always very important in our family. In Louisville, we belonged to Crescent Hill Baptist Church, which was a lovely church. Every time church opened, we were there. On Sunday mornings, we always went to Sunday school and church. Mother sang in the choir with great enthusiasm. My father did, too until he lost his job. He never sang after that – never even hummed a tune. But I remember vividly his strong, baritone voice.

Dad was very active in the church, and a leader in it until the Depression when he lost all his self respect, ego and drive. Dad was very faithful going to church all the time, but after the Depression, he wasn't the church leader like he could have been.

Mother was a different story. She just kept right up prissy-panting around. She had a little net on her head with beads in it and she wore the same shoes for two or three years and they looked brand new.

I'll never forget the time that I dropped the collection plate when I was sitting two thirds back in the church. Everything in the plate rolled all the way down to the front and since it's a big church, it made quite a commotion.

While we were in Shreveport a few years later, we went to the First Baptist Church which was the second largest church in the United States with about 5,000 - 10,000 members. At the time we were going there, M.E. Dodds was the pastor and it was great and the people were great.

I remember going to BYPU, the Baptist Young People's Union. Now it's called something else, but we were very active in that organization. Later on, when I went to medical school in Louisville, with my friend from Baylor, Payton Kolb, we joined Crescent Hill Baptist church. The southern Baptist seminary in Louisville is one of the biggest Baptist seminaries and it's right down the hill from the Crescent Hill Baptist Church so that's where all the seminary students go.

The day that Payton and I joined, there must have been 100 or 150 seminary students who joined at the same time so we got mixed in with the seminary students. They put me down as a preacher student. I was about 20 or 21. I like to tell people that I was a preacher for a while!

Chapter Three

Crawfordsville, Indiana

The Depression changed things for almost everyone. It caused our family, like many others, to make some tough decisions and major changes in how we did things.

After Dad lost his job in Louisville when I was about 11 years old, Mom and Dad came to me and said, "We're going to have to change some things because we can't afford to feed both you and Weston. We think you ought to go live with Aunt Ruth." Aunt Ruth, Ruth Caroline Leisk, was my mother's sister and she was married to George Arthur Collett.

I said, "That's all right." It wasn't a traumatic decision, as I recall, since I'd been in Aunt Ruth's house a lot of times. Going to live with them was just like going home, because we'd been going there so long. We'd go visit them a couple of times a year and stay for several days at a time doing lots of fun stuff like going to Indianapolis and seeing the baseball team there or going to basketball tournaments.

Aunt Ruth and Uncle George lived in Crawfordsville, Indiana which is only about 120 miles from Louisville. Aunt Ruth and Uncle George had four children: Hugh, Jean, Mary Ann, and little Johnny, who was born several years after the others. Mary Ann was the most beautiful baby there ever was and I'd babysit with her and had a hand in raising her. Hugh was a year younger than me and we got along really well. He later became a doctor, too.

In the back row are my father and me. In the front were Jean Collett and Weston.

On the front row were my cousins, Jean Collett and Phyllis Gauss. On the back frow from the left were Weston, Mary Gauss, and me.

Left to right were: Jean Collett, me, Mary Ann Collett, and Hugh Collett in Crawfordsville.

Aunt Ruth and Uncle George lived in Mills Place, on the right side of the railroad tracks, so to speak. They lived in a lovely home with hardwood floors, big bedrooms, fireplaces and a sleeping porch on the back where we used to sleep. It was a two-story home with a basement. Aunt Ruth kept it absolutely immaculate and it was just wonderful. They paid $7500 for the house during the Depression and it infuriated my grandmother that they had paid so much money for the house during such trying times.

Aunt Ruth and Uncle George's house in Crawfordsville, Indiana where I lived two different times. I'm standing on the front porch. The house still stands and is about half a block from Wabash College where my grandson, Gary Paul, went to college.

I lived with the Colletts in Crawfordsville two different times. The first time was when I was about 11 and the second time was when I was a sophomore in high school. In many ways, my two different stints there greatly shaped my life.

It was very comfortable for me to live with my aunt and uncle and their family. After all, they were family. I knew a lot of kids in the neighborhood because I had played with them so many times when we visited my aunt and uncle through the years. They all knew me because I was Dr. Collett's nephew and there was never any of the talk like, "Oh you're just that kid from down south."

I played on all the ball clubs. They just accepted me. I could help the team a little bit and they could help me. It was very easy living there.

I don't remember ever missing my parents, probably because I was so comfortable and happy in Crawfordsville. Mother came to visit me once while I was there. I walked in the living room of my uncle's house and there was a lady sitting there. I just walked right by her. I didn't know her.

Aunt Ruth said, "Dudley, come back here. You just walked by your mother." I had not recognized my own mother. She looked thin and worried and just plain bad. I know now why. It was tough living during the Depression without a job.

It must have really hurt that I didn't recognize my own mother. I can only imagine how difficult those times were for her. You see, her daddy was a captain on the Great Lakes and a boat owner. She had been used to a real high standard of living. My dad had an education – he was smart. But, the Depression didn't discriminate. People lost their jobs and there were no jobs to be had. That's the reason people jumped out of these big office buildings and killed themselves.

Aunt Ruth in her later years

It must have been a terribly demoralizing time for my parents. Life was easy for me, living those two different times with my aunt and uncle. But, it was quite a different story for my parents.

Train Rides

I don't really remember the train trip when I moved in with Aunt Ruth and Uncle George, but I made a lot of train trips by myself, even at a very early age. It was very common for young people to travel on trains by themselves. They had nurses on the train to take care of everybody. When you bought your ticket, you said you wanted to have a nurse or someone to help make connections, and it was arranged.

One train trip I do remember is the trip from Crawfordsville down to Shreveport to see my folks. I was about 12 years old and was going to be traveling by myself, so Aunt Ruth packed some food for me: cookies, sandwiches, apples, oranges and the whole bit. While I was on the train, I was very careful to conserve my food so I'd have enough for the whole trip which took a day and a half. From Louisville, we went down to Jackson, Mississippi and then over to Shreveport.

When I got to Shreveport, I still had a lot of food left. But, before I could even get into the car with my relatives, my &^%$# cousins grabbed my sack. Those crazy kids took off running and they finished off my food as quick as you can imagine. I hollered and screamed and it didn't do any good. It was gone by then. I'll never forget those devils eating all my food.

Weston and me with our cousins on a typical day at the country club. From left: Bruce, Weston, Jean, me and Hugh.

COUNTRY CLUB LIVING

My aunt and uncle belonged to the country club which was VIP stuff. We got to have a milkshakes and hamburgers and boy, that was living in those days!

We went swimming and played a lot of golf. I even played on the golf team for boys up to age 16. There were three of us in that age group. When the men went to another country club in another town to have a golf tournament, we'd go, too. I caddied and did everything.

Once, Uncle George got a letter from the country club saying that he owed so much money because I was playing golf and I wasn't a member of the family. He took me with him to see the golf pro. As we faced that fellow, my uncle said, "Look! As long as Dudley is in my house, he is my son. You leave him alone. Don't you ever charge him and wipe those charges off my bill right now." He considered me his son and that made a big impact on me. I had it all.

FIRST DANCE

The first time I ever danced was the second time I was living in Crawfordsville. Aunt Ruth said, "Dudley, you're going to take this nice girl named Jean to a dance." First I had to learn how to dance so Aunt Ruth taught me right there in the living room. We played the good old music like the songs I like to play today.

But when it was time to go to this particular dance, I was having second thoughts about actually getting out on the dance floor and Aunt Ruth knew it. Before I left to go to the big event, she said, "Now, Dudley. If you don't dance, I'm going to come in and get you and take you home." She wasn't kidding.

My date, Jean, was a honey and a really nice person. We got to the dance and we waited for the music to start. But by then, I was losing my nerve and the girl didn't look so inviting to me. The idea of dancing and holding a girl was just too much.

So I sat around hemming and hawing and talking to the guys. I could tell that she wanted to dance. She was dressed up pretty and I was dressed up pretty good, too. I didn't know what I was going to do until I looked through the window and I saw Aunt Ruth looking right at me. I knew that she meant business.

I said to myself, "Dudley, you'd better get out there and dance or you're getting ready to get jerked out of here and sent home." So, I danced. I put my arm around her and away we danced. After that, I danced with other people, too.

Becoming Interested in Music

Another life-altering event for me that occurred in Crawfordsville was that I got interested in music. There was going to be a state band contest there and they needed ushers in the auditorium, so they asked some of the guys on the football team to do the honors. At the time, I was playing football.

They said, "Boys, we need somebody to usher." They looked around and no one raised their hands. Football players today wouldn't have raised their hands either. But, about three or four of us raised our hands and I was one of them. I thought, "These are nice people. They're talented, too."

There happened to be a band from Hobart, Indiana playing in the contest. William D. Revelli was the director at the time and in fact, he was the greatest college band director in the United States for years. He was later head of the University of Michigan band, but he started in Hobart, Indiana which is a steel mill town. He took that bunch of steel mill workers and they never had to compete in the state contests. They just had to give a concert. They always got sweepstakes.

When I showed up at that band concert which Revelli was directing, I had never heard such music. I thought, *Boy, this means more than playing football and getting the heck beat out of you and having to come home every night sore as the dickens. Basketball's not much better.*

From that moment on, I became involved in music and for the next 70 years or so, it's been a major part of my life.

Uncle George and His impact on My Life & My Career

From the time I was very young, I knew that I wanted to become a doctor. I saw how tough it was for my father when he lost his job. That was probably a big incentive in my decision to become a doctor. When I went to live with my aunt and uncle, I saw that even though the Depression was hitting a lot of people really hard, my uncle was still making a good living as a physician and I had a lot of respect for him. People always need doctors, regardless of the economics of the times.

I saw how Uncle George worked. Day after day, he'd come home at 2:00 or 3:00 in the morning just like doctors do. When he'd come in, he'd sit down at the piano and play that or his flute. He'd operate all day long and then unwind by playing music.

He had a tremendous surgical practice in Crawfordsville which at the time had about 12,000 people. Crawfordsville would kind of remind you of Canyon, in a way. It's a good town with a good college called Wabash College. My grandson, Gary Paul, (Gary & Paula's son) went to college there.

During the lean years, some of Uncle George's patients paid him with food if they didn't have any money. Maybe they paid with chickens or something out of the garden, but they always appreciated what he did for them.

Uncle George was very active in his community and in his profession. He was president of the Indiana Medical Society. There are two representatives from each state for the American College of Surgeons and he was one of the representatives. Now, that ain't bad. He also taught at the University of Indiana medical school at Indianapolis 45 miles away. He was a first class, acceptable doctor.

As an example for community service, Uncle George was tops, too. He taught the Sunday school class at Wabash College every Sunday morning for about 450 men. They don't even hold that class anymore. He also started the Knife and Fork Club wherever he went. Though he wasn't a dynamic speaker, he had a message. When he took the time to talk, you had better listen.

He had a class on medical history in his living room every year with about 15 - 20 premed students. You just went to Dr. Collett's and he'd talk about medical history.

Dr. George Collett, my uncle and a man who had a profound influence on my life.

When I first started thinking about becoming a doctor, my uncle had some advice for me that I'll never forget. He told me, "I don't care where you go, but make sure that wherever you go, there is a university or college – a school of higher learning – because it's a good place to live and you have nice people. And make sure you see Hereford cattle."

He also had some other words of wisdom for me when I was 12 years old – I'll never forget it. He said, "Dudley, if you want to be a doctor, I'm going to tell you two things. Number One is you don't go into medicine to make money. Son, if you do, I'll break your damn-fool neck." He just looked at me and said that.

The second thing he said was, "Remember you don't own anybody." That doesn't mean anything to some people, but it's an important lesson for people in medicine to remember. When I opened my practice several years later, I remembered Uncle George's words. After a patient had been with me for 20 or 30 years, it would be easy to think of them as "my patient." But Uncle George taught me never to take a person for granted as they were free to leave whenever they wanted to. A doctor never "owned" a patient. It's a big lesson. That's one thing that kills doctors worse than anything.

Uncle George was quite a guy and had a profound effect of my life. Because of him, I chose to become a doctor.

Chapter Four

Moving Around

After living with my aunt and uncle for about 18 months, I went back to Shreveport where Dad was working at Barksdale Field. The family supported each other, just like people did. If you didn't have any money, your family took care of you. You took care of the family, too. You did what you could.

The family was very close. Real close. Mother had three sisters and one brother who were all a close family. I think that rubbed off on us, too. When Uncle Will's wife walked out on him one day, leaving him with two babies, my mother, Aunt Jessie and Aunt Ruth took time off and went to his home to take care of those children. They rallied around each other. They didn't ask anyone else, they just did it.

I'm sure that Uncle Will had a hand in getting my father a job working on the construction of Barksdale Field which started in 1931. Barksdale was the largest airfield of its time, covering 22,000 acres. It was where the multi-engine bombers – including the B-17s and B-25s – were stationed. During World War II, it was a crucial training bases for our bomber crews and even trained the 17th Bomb Group led by Gen. Jimmy Doolittle during his raid on Tokyo.

As a side note, when the space shuttle *Columbia* went down in February of 2003, Barksdale Field was one of the NASA collection sites for the shuttle debris.

Ironically, during World War II, I was stationed at Barksdale field for 2 ½ years when I was on active duty. By that time, my brother Weston

Even when I was very young, I often visited with the children of Uncle Will and Aunt Evelyn. I'm in the middle at 21 months with Wardell (left) and Tom Leisk.

Uncle Will with my mother and grandmother.

Mother and Dad in Shreveport, Louisiana where we lived for several years.

had been killed and they wouldn't send me overseas. But, I'm getting ahead of my story...

While we lived in Shreveport, we lived in a nice house, had good friends and went to a good school. Schools meant a lot to us. I played on all the athletic teams there were to play on. I wasn't the big man on campus. I wasn't a big nothin'. I was called "Cousin Four-Eyes" because I wore glasses and couldn't see without my specs. I couldn't play a lot of stuff, but I did enough. I participated. I got along wherever I went. I guess I got a lot of bull, but I never had any trouble.

Whatever it Took

After we lived in Shreveport for awhile, I guess my father lost his job again when the air base was finished. So I went back to live with my aunt and uncle and their family in Crawfordsville. My parents and Weston spent awhile moving from place to place while my dad tried to find enough work to support the family. There wasn't much work during those years.

As kids, we adapted pretty well to moving from place to place, but it must have had an affect on Mom. I'm sure it did, but she had some support from her brother, Uncle Will, who was an oil man living in Shreveport. He made a lot of money and he took care of his four sisters. You didn't like moving, but you did it, because you were just trying to survive.

I remember seeing her crying one day. I'm sure the life she was living with us during the Depression was very different from the one she had been used to when she was growing up on the Great Lakes. She was used to nice things then, but we didn't have them during the Depression.

In Kilgore, I remember my dad had a job for awhile making $65.00/month walking the pipeline. Those were lean years. Though Dad was not working for Shell Oil Company, we lived in the Shell camp in a little two-room shack with a natural gas stove and coal oil lanterns. My cousin Wardell, who was Uncle Will's boy, lived with us for awhile while he was working in the oil field. Five people in two rooms was pretty tight.

The kitchen in our little two-room shack was tiny, only about 50 square feet, but we had an ice box which was filled with ice about once or twice a week. In one of the rooms, there was a one-person bed with a screen across it to lend a little privacy. The other room — which is where I slept with my brother and Wardell when he was there — had a double bed and a couch in it . She always put her children first and gave us the bigger room. That was just the way my mother was.

Of course, there was no air-conditioning. We had a screened in window with a tarpaulin over it. If you pulled the tarp over the window, you'd get cold pretty quick. In the winter, we used little gas heaters.

There was no indoor plumbing and we had to pump our own water. We had to use an outhouse out back and it was a good one.

Lots of Fights

When Weston and I were growing up, I fought with him every day and every night. We had to sleep together in a small bed. I drew an imaginary line down the middle and said, "This is the center of the bed, Bud. Now, don't you come onto my side. If you do, I'm going to beat you up."

Invariably, he'd get over on my side so I'd just knock heck out of him and he'd knock heck out of me. The slats under the bed would come out and we'd fall to the floor. At that point, my Dad would come into our room and say, "Oh no! The boys are at it again!"

When I was about 15 and we were living in Kilgore, we had a fight that I won, but I lost. We didn't have a chifforobe where we could put our clothes, we just had a little mirror on the wall. I was fixing my tie one morning and I kind of prolonged the process, knowing that it was making my brother mad, which was the whole idea.

Weston needed to use the mirror, too so he said, "Get out of the way!" When I didn't, he hit me. To retaliate, I gave him an upper cut to his mouth and I knocked three teeth through his lower lip. They just came right through.

I said, "Boy, that's great. Look what I did to you!" But I looked at my hand and it was bleeding. The dirtiest wound in the world is a mouth wound. I got an infection that went up my arm that lasted for three months. I soaked that arm in hot water with Epsom salts, but it still turned green and the skin sloughed off. You could see all the tendons in it. I was out of school for three months soaking that thing in hot Epsom salts water. We had no antibiotics in those days.

Naturally, my brother rejoiced every day.

Boys Will Be Boys

Like most boys, we did our share of pranks. Our favorite thing to do on Halloween was to pull over all the outhouses in town. Occasionally, there would be a woman inside screaming and hollering, but we wouldn't worry about that. It was a lot of fun. Sometimes, we'd take the outhouse and set it on top of a person's house. If you get three or four boys, you can move an outhouse.

In Kilgore, we stole watermelons or sugar cane. We knew where the watermelon patches were, and five or six of us boys would get two or three

From left: Weston, my father, mother and me at the Shell Camp in 1933 with our two-room shack in the background.

watermelons, never more than we needed. It was great fun to sit close to the gas flares and eat that watermelon.

As for sugar cane, the trouble was that when we ate too much of it, we got diarrhea.

When we lived in Shreveport, two or three times a year we'd put some soap on the street car tracks so the street cars couldn't go up the incline. They'd just sit there and spin the wheels.

Another prank I remember was one we pulled in Louisville where we lived about a block from the railroad tracks. Fine passenger trains went through the city, carrying people back and forth to Cincinnati, New York, Chicago, and Washington D.C.

Those tracks could spoil the plans of people headed for a nice picnic with their friends or family if they made the mistake of putting their food on their car bumpers like many of them did. When the cars went over the railroad tracks, sometimes the food bounced off. We'd get everything that had fallen off and hide it. When people came back looking for their picnic materials, we'd say we hadn't seen anything, then enjoy the feast. Sometimes we would tell them about it, but most of the time we didn't.

School Memories

I went to several different schools during my early years and have some pretty strong memories of a few things. The one teacher who really sticks in my mind was the Latin teacher in Crawfordsville. Boy, she was the meanest white woman I ever saw. She didn't fool with me and that's the reason I liked her. I really respected her. I found out the teachers you didn't like were usually your best teachers. They were challenging the heck out of us and they didn't take any baloney.

I made a jackass out of myself one time when I was taking an etiquette class in school. The subject was how to properly introduce one person to another. My assignment was to introduce one of my friends to some girl in the class who thought she was stuff on a stick. I didn't like her one bit so I was going to show her a thing or two. I introduced her to the colored boy in the class who was my buddy. He was a darn good guy and as far as I was concerned, it was putting him down to say "hi" to her.

Boy she got mad and went out and cried and cried. The teacher took me aside and said, "You should have never done that." All the kids talked about it in school.

My first year of high school in Kilgore was in a big, old, red brick building. I enjoyed school a lot and particularly liked math and science. English classes didn't make much sense to me, but I wasn't bad. I didn't love it, but I was the top boy in my freshman class.

My social life revolved around school, church and music. I played in a band which played for the dances, so I didn't get to do much dancing myself. Music has always been a big part of my life.

During my senior year, I had a girl who I was going "steady" with. That meant I had three dates in one year. I didn't have much time for girls. I was busy working. If I could make $5.00 or a dollar, that was a lot of money.

When I graduated from Kilgore High School, I was third or fourth in the class. I think the reason I fell down in my studies was that I had gotten interested in music by then and I practiced so much that I didn't concentrate on my studies like I could have. But, I did respond to a challenge. When one of my teachers said, "Dudley, we're going to have a contest and I want you to win it," I studied like the dickens and I'd usually win.

I liked typing and shorthand and even entered the interscholastic league contest in those two subjects. I didn't win, but I could breeze by on that typewriter. In those days, typing and shorthand were like what computers are today. A lot of boys and girls took the classes.

THE KILGORE HIGH SCHOOL BAND

When I went to Kilgore High, I was not eligible to play sports because I'd been living in another state (Louisiana). The football coach came to me and said, "Moore, I'd like you to play with us because I know what you can do. But you can't because you're ineligible, so you might as well go do something else."

"Don't come back here," he said. "Go over to the band hall. They always need someone to blow a horn in the band."

Doing just what he said, I made my way to the band hall and I spotted an old bass horn lying in the corner. The band director, Otto Paris, gave the only bass player an order. "Blaze, take Dudley here and teach him the B-flat scale," he said.

That was on a Thursday night. On Friday night, Kilgore played Henderson High School and we played one piece, *Betty Coed*, and it didn't sound the same way twice.

The relationships that I built during those years were long lasting ones. In January of 2003, I went to Huntsville with my sons, Gary, Richard, Bill and Joe and we all visited with Otto Paris. At the time, he was 98 years old and was in the early stages of Alzheimer's disease, but he was sharp as a tack during our visit and what a visit it was!

Early Jobs

When I was a sophomore or junior, we lived in the Shell Oil camp as I mentioned before. My first job was working with the Jeffries Teamsters about 1933. We didn't have paved roads in east Texas then, and with the rains and all the mud, you couldn't use a truck to move the drilling rig equipment. So they had to have mules and teams to do it.

Our band at Kilgore High School with Otto Paris as the band director.

Our tuba section in the Kilgore band was really something. From the left, the tuba players were: me, Edsel Lyon, Weston, and Blaze Gangwere.

Jeffries needed a bunch of mules to do all the work and kept about 1,000 of them in one large pasture. I bummed around in his stables for fun, and one day he asked me if I'd like to count mules for him in the evening.

I said, "Sure would!" As the boss of the Teamsters, he had the best of everything and he let me ride his best horse and use his good saddle. It was hog heaven to me. I'd get on that horse and go about a mile from where his office was, then we'd go through the gate and into a big pasture where the mules were. I guess he had couple of sections of land that he rented or owned.

Once I was in that pasture, I'd just let the horse go and do what he was trained to do. He could lead me to the mules, because he knew where they were supposed to be. I counted as fast as I could as we ran through the pasture for about 20 minutes. We counted those mules every night and the same mules were always in the same places.

I didn't make a penny for that "job." But, I had a lot of fun doing it and I got to ride Mr. Jeffries' horse and use his saddle and that was pretty special.

The first job that I actually got paid for was working at the bus station for the Airline Bus Company in Kilgore when I was about 15. My

Counting mules for Jeffries Teamsters at the Shell Oil camp.

mother made sandwiches and I sold them and I got to keep the profit. Mom would make about a dozen sandwiches and we'd put them in a little case at the bus station. I usually worked from about 6:00 in the evening until the station closed at 9:30 when the last bus came in. Then I closed down the station.

It was pretty good money. I'm guessing I made about $15.00 or $20.00 each week. Mother didn't charge me anything for the sandwich makings, so I got to keep everything I made. She made every kind of sandwich: chicken, ham or bologna, or peanut butter and jelly. The sandwiches were big and they were good. People would get off those busses and be hungry and they'd be happy to buy the sandwiches for about 25¢ each. Sometimes I tried to pay Mom for making the sandwiches, but she always said, "I'll let you know when you owe me some money." That's just how she was.

My first "real" paying job was with Shell Oil Company as a stenographer which was a job I got at the end of my senior year in high school. (In those days, high school only went to the 11th grade.) When I needed a job, I applied for every job in Kilgore. I just wanted to work.

An Evening's Entertainment in Kilgore

When we were living in Kilgore, every night we'd hear guys on the other side of the creek, hollering and screaming and having a good time. One day, we decided that we were going to go and find out what they were doing. We went to the creek bottom where we'd heard the noise coming from and started poking around with some sticks, scraping the leaves around. I said, "Hey, something is here, fellas."

We scraped off the leaves off and raised the top off of a big 3 x 5 metal container buried in the ground. Inside we found a bunch of brown bottles with beer in them. I said, "Hey, these guys have beer down here! They're drinking beer! Let's get them."

So we got some rocks and threw them down there, smashing the bottles. There might have been 100 of them, but probably more like 10 or 20. I don't know. After we got through breaking the bottles, we smoothed all the leaves back over the container. When we were finished, you couldn't tell that anyone had been there.

That night they all came out to have their big shindig — men and women, girls and boys, or whatever you want to call them. Then they started cussing. You could hear every word. They said, "Those &^%$# boys! They've torn up this place…Look what they've done here!"

Boy, we didn't go down that creek bottom for a long time. That was a good experience and a funny one. We just busted all that beer. Just so there's no mistake about it, those guys were bootleggers!

CHAPTER FIVE

Baylor University

Music has always been a big part of my life. I loved to play all kinds of music, and it was a big help to me because it helped pay my way to college. Because of a music scholarship that I got, I was able to go to Baylor University in Waco, Texas and major in premed. I'm not sure where I would have gone, or how my life might have been different if I hadn't gotten a scholarship to go there, because there was no money for college when it was my time to go. But, I had known since I was 12 that I wanted to be a doctor and Baylor seemed like a good place to go.

At the time I started at Baylor in 1936, Baylor had 1,200 students and only 26 of them were majoring in premed. They were all good, hard-working students. All of them wanted to go to medical school as bad as I did.

Too Many Unknowns

One of the courses that I remember was a chemistry class where I had to get 13 "unknowns" in a semester. Basically, they gave you a solution and you had to determine what all of the ingredients were.

The first week, I got five of them and was chugging along pretty well. The assistant in the class rode me pretty hard. He said, "You think you're pretty smart getting five. You probably think you'll be out of this course pretty fast," he said. "Well, you'll never get another one," he predicted.

He was right. For the next three weeks, I didn't get another one. The fellow had diluted the solution so much that you couldn't pick up anything. The head of the chemistry department was Dr. Gooch and he was also my premed advisor. I went into his office and told him I was having trouble with the class. He said, "Let me go see."

So he went into the chemistry class and found the cards telling what was in the unknowns. He looked at them and said, "Dudley, don't worry. You're not going to get another one this semester." And I didn't. He said, "Just keep working and see what you can do."

I worked my tail off, even spending nights up there. It made me so mad that a guy would think I couldn't do the work! It's not that I was mad at him because of what he did, but it challenged me. I made an A in the course.

BAND AT BAYLOR

Everett McCracken was the band director at Baylor when I was there and he was to Baylor what Gary Garner was to me and the West Texas A&M band. Our band at Baylor was the best symphonic band in the state of Texas. We weren't the best *marching band*, though, because of those &^%$# Aggies.

One really bad experience I had in the band had to do with the University of Texas. We were playing a football game in Austin, and Baylor was behind 18 - 0 with 7 minutes to go, but we ended up beating them 21 - 18. I can remember that Billy Patterson threw the passes and Sam Boyd, the end, caught them. Boyd went on later to become a coach.

When we won the game, the Texas students were so doggone mad that they started raising heck with us. They thought that Baylor was just that little place in Waco across the Brazos River. After the game was over, we started playing *The Good Old Baylor Line*, our school song. The rule was when you played the song, you looked directly at the band director.

When we played the song that night, I couldn't look at the director because I had to lean over. The reason I had to lean over was because when we started playing the song, one of the Longhorn fans threw a brick at me and it had knocked me out of my seat. (We didn't have bleachers in

October 27, 1940

Dear Mother:-

    Well home-coming is all over now and we are ready to start studying a bit, that is after we recuperate from this week-end. We all had a good time of course there were many things that were disgusting and that shouldn't have happened but on the other hand there were many good things. The weather was good to us as it rained off and on but never when we had some-thing going on. Just after the parade and the game it poured down but not for a long time. Right now it looks as if it might rain and rain plenty hard. There were quite a few people here for the game and I saw quite a few alumni that I knew. I didn't see any people from either Longview, or Kilgore but perhaps they just weren't around when I was. We guarded the campus every-night but I stayed up only one night and that was enough for me. The parade had many nice floats in it and the band lead that parade. It was an up-hill march and a couple of girls were sick when it was over for we fairly flew up those hills. At the game we had a good place to sit and the game was a honey. A.& M. has a fine team and I believe that the best team did win although ours played a good game. We didn't play inspifed ball but just regular good defensive ball and no offense at all. I still think we need a change in coaching around here cause things that happened in that game and in every game just shouldn't happen at all. There were about 20,000 people there which made the place packed and with the good weather and all we couldn't have asked for more.

    I got along with the two girls okay and kinda think that I like Elaine Meredity a bit the best now. She seems to have a little more sense but that doesn't mean that I'll think that for long cause I believe I had better find me another girl friend and settle the whole proposition. I took Elaine to see "Knute Rockne" and enjoyed it very much and that was my celebration for the week-end. The brass quartet played twice yesterday, once in the intermediate dept. and then last night at the Austin Ave. Methodist Church. We played the "Holy City" last night and did just fairly good as we were not just real confident in ourselves It has a hard French Horn and Trombone part and those to instuzments were lucky to hit just a few of their notes. We road down on a city bus and darned near wrecked the thing with our horns etc. before getting off. The bus driver said that he would not pick us up if he saw us again but I believe he would have done so. I have a thousand and one things to do this week-end and this week so I don't know just where to start. The band may or may not go to T.C.U. game next week which is in Ft. Worth and I am hoping that it doesn't for I need to stay here and study.
    As for what offices etc. I hold I'll think about them and let you know in the next letters There are too darn many of them I know any-way. Well I'd better close and get ready for my 8 O'clock class cause the chimes just rang. Write soong and send some cookies and money if you can. Take care of yourselves.

    Lots of love

Clubs on back

Dudley

A letter that I wrote to my parents while I was at Baylor University.

Pre-Med- Pres. for fall term
Tri-Beta- Historian (Zoology
Phi Mu Alpha- Secretary (music
Boys S.S. Class- Vice Pres.
B.T.U. - Lead singing
Band- manager & gen. flunky

game costs $2.50

These were the clubs that I was in while I was at Baylor University.

The Baylor band, with Everett McCracken as the director. Four of our saxophone players were quadruplets named Key. I'd bet not many bands have that!

those days; there were just boards.)

Worse that getting knocked out of my seat was that when the brick hit my horn from behind, the force had jammed the mouthpiece into my lips and I was bleeding pretty good. I saw Mr. McCracken coming up through the band.

All he knew was that I hadn't been watching him when I played the song. He said, "Moore, you're out of the band. Turn your uniform in." When I opened my mouth to say something to him, the blood just poured out. That bass horn mouthpiece had made a deep cut in a perfect circle around my mouth.

When he asked me what had happened, I pointed to the brick that was next to me. He said, "My God, you're lucky to be alive. They just barely missed your head, didn't they?"

The first thing Mr. McCracken did was call the police and say, "Get our busses on the football field right in front of the band. We're not going to walk out of this stadium."

They drove the busses right onto the grass, put them right in front of us, and we got in. Then we went down to the depot, got on the train and came home. But boy, the cut inside of my mouth was bad. It took it about a month to heal and it was a while before I could play my horn.

It was lucky the guy's aim was off because if the brick had hit me in the head instead of hitting my horn, I'd have been a dead duck. That's the reason I don't like the University of Texas to this very day. They're so &^%$# smart. So good. So big. So dominant. I don't like anything about them. I understand the person who threw that brick was just one person and being a Christian, I should forgive him and all that stuff, but that just got me.

Another vivid memory that I have from my band days was the time that my parents came to Tyler to watch me play during the Baylor and Centenary College game. We rode the Cotton Belt train from Waco to Tyler and when I stepped off the train, there was my mother standing there. She was so proud to see me! All my dad said to me at first was, "Hi, Boy."

We talked for a few minutes, but it got time for the game so I said,

"Mom, I've got to go into the stadium now. Where are you folks sitting?"

Dad said, "Son, we're sitting out here on the bench because we don't have any money to go to the game."

I wish that I had had enough money to pay for their tickets, but I didn't. I was at Baylor on a scholarship, and if it hadn't provided me with 75¢ to eat on, I wouldn't have had money for food. This was 1936 or 1937 and it's probably hard for my grandkids to realize that times would be so tough you wouldn't have an extra dollar or so, but that's the way it was.

A Variety of Musical Roles

While I was going to school at Baylor, I played not just in the Baylor symphonic band, but also in the Waco symphony as a tuba player. We also had what we called the Holy Four. It was a brass choir that played religious music for various events on campus. We had a trombone, baritone, French horn, and of course the bass. One of the best things that I ever did was get up on top of Waco Hall and play Christmas carols. It was beautiful.

We also played for memorial services and for churches all through the area, including the little town of Clifton, a little Lutheran community just west of Waco.

In our brass choir, the Holy Four, we were (from left) me, Payton Kolb, James Ratteree and Paul Hollinger.

At Baylor, I was a member of BYPU, but in that environment the nickname for the organization was "Button Your Pants Up." On Sundays, I always went to Sunday school during the day, then went to BYPU at night.

One night, I was sitting with a girl named Mary Jane Laughlin and all 200 or so BYPU members were singing our favorite songs. Our singing leader was a ministerial student. There was nothing I hated worse than ministerial students because they always married the good-looking girls, and they always had money because they got paid to preach in the country churches. Those devils.

Anyway, as we sang, I made note of the song leader's skills or lack thereof. After a while, I said to Mary Jane, "If I couldn't do any better than that, I would sit down."

She said, "Can you do better?"

I said, "Sure can."

So she laughingly said, "Then you've got the job next Sunday night." For the next three years, I led the singing at Baylor in Sunday school and church. Then the director didn't show up for the night service, so they just took me out of the audience and asked me to lead the singing. It was a big church, but I said, "OK," and led the singing. Ever since then, I've led singing wherever I went.

A BREAK IN MY COLLEGE EDUCATION

I went to Baylor for two years, but after my second year, the financial director, John Jolly, asked me *not* to come back to Baylor because I owed them so much money. They wrote me a letter and said, "Dudley, when you pay your bill, you can come back and go to school." That's when I got a job working on freighters on the Great Lakes.

CHAPTER SIX

Freighters on the Great Lakes

After I got the news that I couldn't go to Baylor any more, I wrote to my Uncle Andrew. He was married to my Aunt Jessie, Mom's oldest sister, and was a captain for Bethlehem Steel. Uncle Andrew had been a sailor for many years, sailing from Norway to South America on his first voyage when he was only 12 years old. He told me that he could remember seeing sailors all over the boat who were dying of malaria.

In my letter, I told Uncle Andrew that I really needed a job, but asked him not to lay anybody off to give me one.

He said, "I'll see what I can do, but I'm not going to fire someone so you'll have a job."

Several in my family sailed on the Great Lakes in the Lackawanna.

This was about 1938 and it was hard to get a job in those times. There were no jobs from about 1932 - 39. I had worked in Shreveport driving a dry cleaning and laundry truck and made $35.00 all summer. You don't go far on $35.00.

At the time I wrote to Uncle Andrew, he was one of three uncles who were captains on the lakes. I also had three cousins who were working on the lakes, so it was very much a family affair.

Uncle Andrew eventually found me a job and I took the train up to Buffalo, New York where Aunt Jessie and Uncle Andrew lived. While I worked on the freighters, I lived with them and paid rent based on how much I was making. They had two sons, Marty and Dick. Dick became a doctor and Marty was sort of a literary genius.

Anyway, I worked on the *Bethlehem* until the boat got laid up in November because of the ice in the lakes and the rivers.

I lived with Aunt Jessie and Uncle Andrew when I wasn't working on the freighters.

When that happened, I spent the winter working on the winter gangs. The boats tied up in the harbor in Buffalo where there were great big grain elevators just everywhere. The boats had corn, wheat and grain on board from their last trip, and they stayed in the harbor until the grain elevators got empty enough to take the grain off the boat. Everything had to be done by hand and it was tougher than heck.

The winters were horribly cold in Buffalo with lots of snow and ice. A big wind would come up from Toledo – then across Lake Erie to Buffalo – and all the boats would rise three or four feet because the water would rise.

In the middle of the night, you had to go out there and let all the

Uncle Andrew on the deck of the Lackawanna.

The Lebanon *negotiating through the ice.*

big heavy cables out by hand then tie the boat up and keep it tied up or you'd break the cables. The next day, the wind would blow the other way and the boats would go down so you'd have to take up the slack. I'd lose two or three sets of gloves every week because I'd grab a cable and then throw it out. The gloves would freeze to it and come off my hands. So, I'd carry an extra pair or two of gloves, even for just an eight-hour shift.

You couldn't be afraid of heights and work on those ships. Sometimes I'd be 75 feet or more above the ship, cleaning the mast. I never looked down; I just kept scrubbing. It wasn't that bad.

In the spring when the thaw started, the boat was filthy dirty because it had been sitting near the

Me working on the mast of the Lackawanna.

steel mill with all that soot, iron dust and red ore. We had to get all that cleaned off, too.

LIFE ONBOARD SHIP

It took us 4 ½ - 5 days to go from Buffalo to Duluth, Minnesota which was one of our typical runs. We'd only be in port about five or six hours, just long enough to unload the boat.

Our living quarters on the ship were pretty cramped. We had six guys in a room that should have had one or two. The cabins had three bunks on each side with a little old wash basin in the corner. Fortunately, we never had six in the room at once because at least one was always working.

The ships had three deck hands, three deck watches, three watchmen and three wheelsmen. (I was a watchman in those days.) The chain of command goes: deck hand, deck watch, watchman, wheelsman, then first mate, second mate, third mate and captain, plus a few other hands. Rounding out the crew, there were 36 men on board at all times – about half in the forward end and half in the aft end.

Believe it or not, I liked everyone I worked with, especially the officers who were all good men. We got along fine. Some of the others were just crum-bums who had girlfriends in every port or wives they'd divorced, but were trying to skip paying alimony to. But everyone minded their own business and they did their jobs well.

There were always one or two college boys on board who were my buddies. I worked really hard and would often take someone else's shift if they wanted to go to shore and had the duty. If it was my time to go ashore and a guy wanted to go in my place, I'd work for him and make $4.00 or $5.00 for working four hours. That was pretty good money in those days. I could do that six or seven times and have enough money for train fare back to see my family in Texas.

It would be stretching the truth to say that it was fun work, but it was a good job. I was beginning to study for my mate's papers. I just think that steamboating was in me. I loved it. Sometimes I'd get seasick when the boat got to rolling, but I learned to get over that foolishness.

For one whole summer, I was a wheelsman and I loved it. It wasn't easy. It's not easy to turn the wheel, but it was fun making things work.

While we were on the ship, we worked two four-hour shifts every day. We worked four hours on and eight hours off. I liked the 2:00 - 6:00 a.m. shift because at that hour of the morning, there was nobody to bother you. I could sneak in the kitchen and get all I wanted to eat.

As part of my early morning duties, I had to get the fire real hot by 5:00. We used hard coal in the big stoves, which had to be so hot that the top was scarlet red all the way across. If it wasn't scarlet red, the skipper and the steward would chew you out. Plus, you had to have the coffee pot steaming when the steward came on at 6:30.

The food was the bonus. It was just wonderful. You'd go in the big refrigerator – which was as big as a good-sized room – and there would be 300 lb. blocks of ice in there. Inside, among other things, would be huge sides of beef. The beef hung in there for three weeks and would become covered with green mold as the enzymes started working. But if you shaved off the mold, the meat was the best in the world.

We got fed three meals a day, but we could get food anytime we wanted. We could also have leftovers like the steaks, the cut meats and the pies. I loved it all. And anytime we wanted, we could just ask the cook to make some eggs and bacon and he'd do it.

EXCITEMENT ON THE RIVER

I'll never forget when we were on the an old tub called the *B. Limon Smith*. The sailors . . . oh, they were something. One of the mates who taught me more than anybody was on that boat. The captain was a skilled man, but he was drunk much of the time. His wife was on the boat with him all the time and they had a son who was a deck hand.

This particular time, we were going into the St. Mary's River to get to the Soo Locks which are between Lake Huron and Lake Superior. It was so foggy, you couldn't see anything, but we could hear the foghorns of the other boats. *Toot, toot, toot* . . . the horns wailed from the boats that had anchored safely at the entrance to the river.

The Soo Locks in the very early years.

The Stewart J. Cort *is one of Bethlehem Steel's "super ships" and is seen here as it passed through the Soo Locks.*

I said to no one in particular, "We're going to drop the hook here pretty soon." They called the whole crew out and we gathered around the captain. He said, "I know my way up this river. I can do it with my eyes shut." And he could. The only trouble with him was that he got drunk about three times a month. That's what ruined him with some of the other companies.

He said, "I'm going to station all you fellows around the boat and I want you to watch carefully and report anything you see. Anytime you see a light, that'll be a buoy. I want you to tell me the color of the light you see from the buoy and I want to know the pitch of the *ping, ping ping*." All of the buoys had bells on them and he knew the pitch of the bells on every buoy. As we started slowly up the river, we made our reports to him.

I'd say, "I hear a high pitch over on the starboard side about 45 degrees off the bow."

The captain replied, "Yep, it ought to be there. Is there a light?"

"Well, I don't see it...Yes, I do, it's red," I told him.

"That's it," he said.

We went up that St. Mary's River for about six hours. It's narrow and rocky and we went up that sucker about a third as fast as we ought to go – probably about two or three miles an hour. We couldn't see anything, the fog was so thick.

I could hear people on the shore talking, but I couldn't see them. They were summer visitors who had their cabins out there and I'd holler at them and they'd holler back at us. We were no more than about six feet away from them because in some places the river was that narrow.

"Where are you?" we asked them and they wondered where *we* were.

We went up that river in the fog with all the twists and turns of the river until we got up to the Soo Locks and the captain blew the horn for the locks to be opened.

I heard one guy say, "What crazy so-and-so is out there in a boat? We want them all stopped!"

Well, we were the crazy so-and-so's he was talking about. The captain blew the horn again, then demanded, "Give me an answer!"

And the people at the locks said, "What are you doing out there?" But, they opened the locks and let us through.

We weren't far from where another boat had sunk about five hours north of the locks. The boat was a beautiful boat and it was coming from Duluth when the waves were too big and too long for the boat and it just broke in two. The whole crew was lost.

But I wasn't afraid that time on the *B. Limon Smith*. I guess I just had confidence in the captain.

The *B. Limon Smith* had a wooden pilot house that had been added on to it. Once when we were on Lake Michigan, we weren't loaded and we were light in the water. We were on our way to Escanaba in Michigan's Upper Peninsula to load some iron ore. We had unloaded coal and the boat was filthy dirty so we were washing the deck off with big fire hoses that were so big it took two people to hold them.

In a storm, you like to have a load in you so you get lower in the water. If you're light, you just bubble around on the surface of the water.

This voyage, we were headed straight into a storm. It was getting darker and the waves were getting bigger and bigger. The old man (the captain) ordered us to go tie the hatches down because no one wanted them to blow off. The boat was rolling pretty severely when all of a sudden, I heard a thud and heard the captain holler, "Get down between the hatches! It's comin'!"

I crouched down between the hatches with my arm locked around a clamp, holding on for dear life. About that time, a huge wave smashed into the pilot house, knocking the wooden structure clean off the boat. I peaked around and there was a wheelsman holding onto the wheel. The mate who was up there with him was holding onto the compass thing and here was this pilot house floating down off the top of the boat, riding the waves.

Somehow the guys who had been in the pilot house made it and got on the boat before the pilot house floated off behind us. We finished

May 28, 1939

Dear Mother:—

Well this is the 5th Sunday that I have been on the boat & what a Sunday. We got into Sandusky, Ohio, at 2 a.m. this morning for our first load of coal & we deck-hands worked from that time until 5:30 p.m. which gives me a good excuse to be tired. It was not real dirty coal but since it was warm today it was bad enough. I wheeled last nite from 10–1 a.m. so I had but one hour's sleep during 24 hours so I am bound to sleep good to-night. We are going to Milwaukee & should get there 5 a.m Wednesday & be out about mid-night. I am going to call up Aunt Frances the first thing. We will most likely paint all day but get part of the night after supper off.

In Buffalo I went out to Aunt Jessie's & the place is beautiful — but! I had the usual talk with Grandma & she seemed fine but discontented as usual. Dick was in his usual mood & Hugh & I had a good time talking about the farm & playing horse-shoes. He is going with Dick, Uncle Andrew on the Wenner which is one of the best little boats in the line. I spent 4 hours out there & came back & worked fairly hard sweeping sticky iron ore. We will be back in Buffalo around Monday with limestone but I do not believe I'll go out to the house. We will also get paid in Milwaukee & I will send my check

I wrote this letter to my mother in 1939.

to you & be sure & send me some orange blank checks for I want to pay for my suit-case. I got me a letter from Mr. Jolley & he said that I was short $78.10 on my bill, but he did not have the $90 check that was sent in October. I have answered him & if there is no trace of it we will send him another one & I will have $12 for next year at school.

I hope to get a letter from you at Detroit in the morning telling me about the concert etc. Write about once every four or five days for that should get a letter to Detroit for the boat each time. Malis as close as can be said. Grandma gave me a snap-shot of you & Dad & you both looked fine. You looked real nice & some of the fellows say that they can see a resemblance between Dad & I.

It is getting late so I will close. I hope that you enjoyed the concert & are getting along all right with your orchestra. You surely are keeping the yard clean but do better with the chickens. Possibly moving the coops & cleaning the grass from them will help. Don't work too hard and feed "the old man & get him fat". Say hello to Josh.

Love to all

Your son
Dudley

the trip using the old pilot house which was below the one that had been added on.

Another time, a fellow had a narrow escape with death when a huge wave hit while he was on the deck. By God, the hand was washed off the boat and into the water. We thought we'd lost him, but another wave came by and washed him back onto the boat. It was amazing!

Even in the summer time, the water in Lake Superior is so cold that if you're in the water more than three or four minutes, you can freeze to death. That fellow wouldn't have survived long in the water.

Another time we were in south Chicago and were just getting ready to leave the dock when someone came running up to the captain and said, "Don't go out there. The Coast Guard said it's going to be rough."

The captain said, "OK. If they say stay, we'll stay," so we put the boat into reverse and tied up. The winds were blowing something fierce. Along came a ship right by us down the Chicago River and I heard my captain holler at him and say, "You're not supposed to go. We're not going."

The man on the other ship yelled back, "I've got a brand new ship and it'll take anything the lakes have to offer," and he kept going. When he was barely 200 yards away, we heard a sound like a cannon exploding. That boat had cracked in two. Fortunately, it didn't break totally apart, but the captain had to keep his nose to the storm, put the boat in reverse and come back into port. He had cracked his brand-new boat right in two. He'd been warned not to go.

I remember another time we were leaving Erie, Pennsylvania and in 24 hours we only made one mile. We were bucking a pretty good head wind. We chugged along for several hours and were still looking at the same place on the shore.

When I worked on the freighters, the water in Lake Superior was so pure that we could take the water right from the lake and drink it. It was blue, pristine and pretty as could be.

But Lake Erie was a different story. It was like a sewer because Detroit and everyone else emptied junk into it. One of the rivers around there would burn if you threw a match on it because of all the paint and chemicals that had been dumped into it. Now, they've cleaned up all that. One of the big paint companies had a big plant there, and you could see the stuff coming out of their sewer works. Yellow, green and any color of paint just floated around on the top of the river. It was disgusting.

Not "Just Sailors"

Once when my cousin, Marty, and I were working on a freighter together at the Soo Locks, we had put ashore to handle the cables. As we were doing our work, we had a long, detailed discussion about the merits of Mozart's music compared to Chopin's. As was common when the freighters put ashore, several people gathered around to watch the activities and some of the people overheard our discussion.

One of them said, "You guys are "just sailors" aren't you?"

We said, "We're sailors."

The fellow said, "It's so surprising to hear you two talking with such knowledge about fine music."

We delighted in telling them – and perhaps changing their perceptions about "sailors" – that I was a premed student and Marty was a law student. They were just floored!

Chapter Seven

Back to Baylor, Then On to Medical School!

After I worked on the freighters for a couple of years, I had saved enough money to go back to Baylor and finish college. I wrote Baylor a check for a little over $800, then presented them with another check for the following year.

But, I wasn't through with the boats. After I graduated from Baylor in 1941, I spent another summer on the boats which helped pay for my first year of medical school.

Laying the Groundwork for Medical School

My first year at Baylor, I went to see the premed advisor, Dr. Gooch, who asked me what my hobbies were. I told him that I played in the band and was on a music scholarship.

He said, "You will never be recommended for med school if you play in a band. You won't have time for it."

I said, "I've got to play in the band because it pays for my tuition and other things, and I work for board in the kitchen at Baylor." Knowing that he was the one who would have to eventually write my recommendation to medical school, I also said, "If I make the grades, you've got to write the recommendation."

He looked me right in the eye and said, "No, I don't."

That devil held that over me for the whole four years I went to Baylor. He'd come by once in a while during the school year and say,

"You remember, Dudley, I'm not going to recommend you for med school."

I said, "But you've got to." The whole time I was at Baylor, I racked up good grades and when the time came to apply to medical school, I went up to him and told him that it was time to write my letter of recommendation. He said, "I told you I wasn't going to write one."

I said, "You have to write one because I've got good enough grades and you know I've worked hard." He told me he'd think about it.

About a week later, he came up to me and said, "Dudley, I mailed that letter up to the University of Louisville. I don't know why I wrote it, but you won't get in on it."

Of course, I got accepted. I wasn't really worried that Dr. Gooch wouldn't write the recommendation. If he hadn't done me right, I would have gone straight to Pat Neff's office. He was the president of the university at the time. Not that I'm mean, but I had to go to medical school and I wasn't going to be cheated.

The Acceptance

The University of Louisville was the only medical school that I applied to. My roommate at Baylor was Payton Kolb. We were good friends and played in the band together. Payton's father, a psychiatrist, had gone to medical school at the University of Louisville so that's where Payton planned to go. I thought that sounded pretty good, so I elected to go there, too and didn't consider going anywhere else. That was about the time that Baylor Medical School was being moved from Dallas to Houston. Even though I might have gotten into Baylor Medical School, I would have lost a year while the school was being moved.

All this happened after Pearl Harbor was bombed in 1941 and I knew that if I didn't start medical school that I was going flat dab into the army.

After I graduated from Baylor in 1941, I spent another summer on the lakes then headed to Louisville with Payton where we started medical school in the fall of 1941. After I got there, I asked the dean of admissions, Dr. Johnson, how the medical school had picked me. After all, it was a

My parents were very proud when I graduated from Baylor University.

municipal school financed by the city of Louisville. I wasn't from Louisville and didn't live in Kentucky.

He said, "Just a minute," then he went to the file drawer and pulled out the letter of recommendation from Dr. Gooch. "Look at this," Dr. Johnson said.

I read it and it was very convincing. Dr. Gooch had said in essence, "This is a man you want to have in your medical school." Dr. Johnson told me that the first one on the admitting committee read the letter, then he passed it around the room for everyone to read. They all said, "Let's take him."

So the man who had threatened me for years ended up writing a pretty convincing letter. Every year for 15 or 20 years, I went to the Baylor University homecoming. Every time I saw Dr. Gooch there, he'd just give me a little salute, scraping his finger along his nose.

MEDICAL SCHOOL AT THE UNIVERSITY OF LOUISVILLE

Needless to say, I was pretty excited to be accepted into medical school and to be one of 100 students in the class. Anyone who has ever been to medical school can attest to the fact that it is very tough. We completed a year's curriculum in nine months. The day after we completed the "year's work," we started on the following year's program. It was pretty grueling and there was no such thing as a summer vacation. But, we did find time for a little diversion occasionally.

One of our favorite pranks was pretty gruesome, so if you're squeamish...go on to the next paragraph! Occasionally, we'd have a bunch of premed students come to visit our campus at the University of Louisville. They always wanted to tour the medical school, so we'd get some bologna and put it down in the cadaver we were dissecting. When those college kids came through, we'd pick the bologna out of the cadaver and eat it. Our professors just groaned.

My good friend, Payton Kolb, and I work on one of the cadavers.

A NEW PHASE – MARRIAGE!

When I was in medical school in Louisville, I met a woman named Doris Compton who was a medical records librarian and a darn good one. After an operation was over, she'd be waiting to take the dictation about the surgery from the best doctor in Kentucky. Boy, she was efficient! That doctor performed an average of six cases a day out of two operating rooms. She did all his dictation. She was sharp – a class act – and I enjoyed getting to know her.

Doris had a lot of personality. People liked her. I knew some girls who went to high school with her and they told me that Doris had been "the most" this and "the most" that and she won every popularity type contest. I enjoyed being with her.

Of course, when you're in a hospital as an intern or a resident, you don't run around town looking for people. You're busy working your tail off. But, she was very nice. Later, too late, I learned that her mother was a very different kind of person from me and that Doris had a very, very severe inferiority complex. When someone has an inferiority complex, you're wiped out right there. Anything you do shows them up and they don't like it.

After we'd been going together a long time, I just let her know that I enjoyed being with her and I thought we ought to consider getting married. And she did, too. It was about like that. We talked a lot about things.

The office where she worked had the best surgeons in the whole state of Kentucky and they all came to the wedding. I thought I made the right decision.

We got married in Louisville in 1945 when I was in my first year of general surgery residency at St. Joe Infirmary. Probably 15 people or so came to the wedding ceremony which was held in the home of the Presbyterian minister who married us.

After the ceremony, we took an airplane to Chicago where we had dinner at the Edgewater Beach Hotel with two of my cousins, Hugh and Dick, and their wives. I remember that dinner was a gift from my Uncle George and after dinner, we listened to a fabulous band on the order of Guy Lombardo's. It was wonderful!

DANCE HALL EMERGENCY

When I was on call in the emergency room as a senior medical student in Louisville, we got word that someone had been shot in a predominently black dance hall. I didn't want to go down there. I just kind of sat back and ignored the news, but the head resident said, "Moore, go ride in the ambulance and see about that fellow."

Grabbing my medical bag, I headed out in the ambulance. When we arrived at our destination, two great big black men came out to meet us. They said, "You stay right with us and you'll be fine." In every Negro community, there is the chief honcho and there are his bodyguards. Well, there must have been 1,000 Negroes in this monster-sized dance hall. All these Negroes had been dancing and having a big time until the guy got shot. There he was, this dead guy lying right there on the dance floor. All of the people with their big, wide eyes were staring at us, and I was scared to death because I was the only white guy. But I stayed close to those two big honchos.

I was so scared! I must have looked so white walking amongst all those Negroes, all of them emotionally upset. You would have thought in that kind of situation, one or two of the crazy big old bucks would have laid into me because I was a white man, but I had those big black fellas right next to me all the way.

When I bent over to examine the body, there was a little blood by the collarbone and sure enough he was dead. The bullet that killed him went in right under the collarbone, hitting a subclavian artery that went to his arm. He bled to death, internally.

During my exam, I opened his eyes and looked in his mouth and saw that the son-of-a-gun had ten diamonds in his teeth – five on the bottom and five on the top. They glistened. They sparkled. The body guard said, "Doctor, you should have seen him when he was up and about. When he flashed his smile, he'd just sparkle."

We put him in the ambulance and the bodyguards came out and got in, too. The whole time, they stayed right by the body – even coming right into the emergency room where all the doctors examined the body again and filled out the paper work. Those guys were like shadows.

Next we shoved the body into the cooler to keep him until the autopsy was done. Those two black guys stood right there, right outside the cooler. When it was time to perform the autopsy, the bodyguards dressed in gowns, gloves, and masks and stood right there by the body during the whole process. They didn't do anything, but they dressed just like we did.

We did the autopsy and closed the body up and every once in a while, we'd look at those teeth and sure enough, there were 10 diamonds there. Can you believe that? Afterwards, we put the body into a hearse and the bodyguards climbed in next to the body. I asked, "Why do you guys stay so close?"

They said, "We don't want anything to happen to those

diamonds," and they drove off in the hearse. I guess they thought someone might take a hammer and just pop out the teeth with the diamonds in them. They were big ones, too! That was the darndest thing I ever did.

MA PICKETT

While I was in medical school, a 69-year old woman named "Ma Pickett" was the head of the OB-GYN department. She was a great OB doctor. Each year, she invited some of the medical students to go with her to the country club dance. While I was in medical school, she picked me and two or three others to go with her as her dates. It was really first class, and she was a real sweetheart.

Ma Pickett had a pair of glasses that would fall down on her nose. I was out on the dance floor with her and we were dancing when this young couple walks up to us. The woman said, "Hello, Dr. Pickett." Dr. Pickett didn't recognize her from anybody and the young woman said, "Don't you remember me? You delivered me."

Ma Pickett said, "Honey, I never saw your face."

Whew! They just danced off and Ma Pickett just kept dancing with me. She was a real character.

She chewed us out one time because we didn't dress properly on Saturday morning to a class that she taught. She gave us holy heck. She said, "You're going to be doctors and you need to dress properly. You look like a bunch of bums off the street." When she talked, we took notice!

POLIO AND THE IRON LUNG

When I was going to school, I worked at Louisville General Hospital. This was in the 1940s and polio had reared its ugly head. We had 20 some-odd iron lungs going the entire time at the hospital. I'll never forget the sound of those machines going *shhhh . . . psssss . . . shhhh . . . psssss . . . .* At the hospital, there were entire rooms filled with those iron lungs, which were like air compressors and were big enough for a person to lie in.

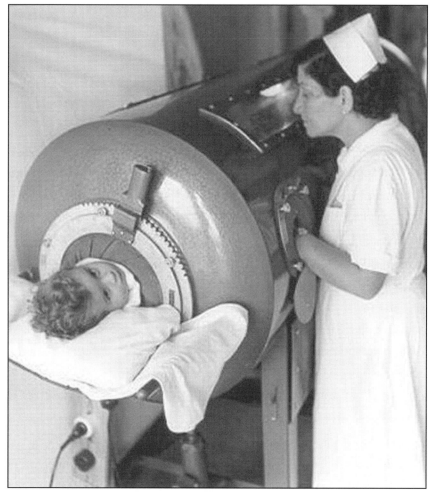

These iron lungs were very common when polio was an epidemic in the United States. (Photo made available courtesy of the World Health Organization)

It was tough.

If someone got bulbar polio, the disease affected everything above the neck and into the brain stem. When that happened, the person died and you couldn't do anything to stop it. (The bulbar part of the brain is the back part.)

Then a hot pack treatment was developed by a nurse from Australia named Sister Kinney. She found that if you wrapped the extremities of polio patients in a warm wool blanket, the arms or the legs wouldn't get stiff. This "Sister Kinney treatment" couldn't stop the polio process, but it could keep a person from becoming deformed.

So we used old GI blankets which we put into real hot water, wrung out, then placed on the patient's arms and legs. When the blankets got cool, we changed them.

About every two beds, there was an old wringer washing machine with boiling hot water inside. Continuously, night and day, the nurses labored to keep warm, wet blankets on the polio patients. There was no antibiotic for polio and this was before the vaccine. Of course, no medicine helped polio. But the vaccine prevented it. You just built up resistance.

Whether someone left the iron lung depended on the amount of damage they had. My job as an orderly was to clean the place up and take care of all the mess. I didn't worry that I would get polio, because no one else was worried about it. We had separate isolation buildings for patients with meningitis and encephalitis and other contagious diseases, but I never knew of anyone getting polio.

Another vivid memory I have about polio was going to the Hialea race track in Florida with my Aunt Ruth. There we saw a specially-equipped big, black hearse. It held a wealthy man named Fred Sipes whose body had been ruined by polio. That hearse housed his iron lung, and had mirrors positioned all around it so Fred could watch the races from the hearse. It was something to see, but we were overcome by the tragedy of the situation.

Intensive Training in Anesthesia

When I was a senior medical student, they needed five senior students who were interested in being anesthetists or surgeons and I was one of them they picked for the anesthesia program. All the anesthetists who had been studying anesthesia in medical school before us had been taken into the armed services. The head of the anesthesia department was named Dougal Dollar and he was a great teacher. He was 60 or 65 and he was the only one who didn't go into the service. He was too old. Until we got trained, he was the only anesthetist at Louisville General Hospital and had to cover a whole string of operating rooms by himself.

He was a great doctor and he was with us all the time. I don't know how he did it. Whenever we were doing cases at that big charity hospital – night or day – he was around. I don't know where he slept or if he slept, but he was nice.

All I did my senior year was give anesthetics – some 8-10 times a day for a year – so we got real good anesthesia training. He taught us how to handle all sorts of emergencies: resuscitations, people in shock, people who were dying on the table. You just had to do what you could to keep them going. That gave me the experience and confidence to handle just about anything.

Later, when I did my internship at St. Joe Infirmary, we rotated through different departments. Often, I'd be on another rotation and someone would come in and say, "Tell Dudley to come up here. I need him right now." Because of the shortage of anesthetists, and because of my excellent training at Louisville General Hospital, I got called to give a lot of anesthesia.

That kind of experience got me a residency in general surgery a few years later. Nobody had a chance to get the residency except me. There were 15 residents originally, but the surgical residency all pyramided down to one – me. No one else stood a chance. I knew all the surgeons because I'd worked with them and had given anesthesia to their patients. They knew the kind of work that I did so I got the residency. But first the service intervened . . .

CHAPTER EIGHT

IN THE ARMY NOW

Like many other people, I'll never forget December 7th, 1941. It was my first semester of medical school and we were sitting in the rooming house where I was living at the time. It was just like September 11, 2001 when the terrorists attacked the World Trade Center in New York. It was exactly the same kind of feeling. People were in shock everywhere and their heads were in a tailspin because the whole world was in turmoil.

Immediately, everything changed. They put us in the army in a program called ASTP, Army Specialized Training Program. For the first three or four months, we were in a reserve unit and didn't wear uniforms. But, after that, we were "officially" in the ASTP program with an attachment and a commanding officer. Then we wore army uniforms. Actually, there was no special army training for us. Our training was to become doctors and serve in the war.

Initially, we worked in the induction center where 1,500 men a day came in to be drafted. We were in the hills of Kentucky and we had a lot of hillbillies come in. They couldn't spell, they didn't know their full names. We'd say, "Where were you born?" Half of them told us they were born at the corner store. No doctors. No nothing.

I suspect many of them were bootleggers or moonshiners.

After my internship at St. Joe Infirmary, World War II was in full swing and doctors were badly needed. Initially, I had wanted to join the Navy in their B-12 program, but when I went to the Navy recruiting station, I had a little problem. My eyesight was too bad. The guy wanted me to read the eye chart. I said, "Where is the chart," then went up and touched it with my hand and stepped back.

He took my by the arm and said, "Come on, Boy. I want to get you out of here before you run into the door." My eyesight has never been good. All the kids in the family called me "Cousin Four-Eyes," but it worked out OK. A lot of people have problems and my eyes were good enough for the army.

MY BROTHER, THE PILOT

I'll digress just a little here to talk about my brother, Weston.

When my brother was 14 years old, he learned to fly an airplane. He just snuck off and did it. I was in Crawfordsville at the time.

When he was just 16 years old, he was a flight instructor in Kilgore, Texas when my family lived there. I don't know how he did it. My parents knew he was doing it and he hadn't killed himself yet, so they let him just keep going. He wanted to go into the air corps. I think he must have been predestined to fly because he had a birthmark in the shape of an airplane on his right shoulder. His love of flying is what killed him.

My brother had a birthmark similar to this one.

When I finished working on the boats on the Great Lakes, I took a Missouri Pacific train down to Longview, Texas. My brother was there to meet me because he was going to take the same train down to Randolph Field in San Antonio. We spoke for a few minutes and he went on to San Antonio. That was the last that I ever saw him alive.

WESTON ANSWERS HIS CALL TO DUTY

Weston went into the service about 1941 or 1942 and was trained at Enid, Oklahoma, Foster Field near Victoria, and at a couple of other bases including a new base in Ft. Wayne, Indiana. He got a new B-26 bomber. I'm sure that Weston was one of our country's finest bomber pilots.

In late 1942, he called me from Florida about 6:00 or 7:00 one Sunday morning. You could hear the motors revving up in the background.

He said, "Bud, I'm going overseas now and with the record of this airplane, I'm not coming back. But I want you to know that I'm doing *exactly* what I want to do. I'm happy, I've got a brand new plane and a good crew and in just a few minutes we're going to fly to Natal, Brazil."

He gave our family a precious gift when he made that call. It gave us the reassurance that he was doing exactly what he wanted to do and was OK with whatever the consequences would be. He also said, "My bank account has been put in your name. If you need any money to go to school, just write a check, Bud."

From Florida, his squadron was going to refuel in Brazil then head to the Ascension Islands out in the Atlantic. Then they flew to Africa and flew up the coast of Africa until they got into conflict near the Suez Canal.

At the time, German Field Marshall Erwin Rommell and his troops were bringing supplies across the Mediterranean from Italy and taking them on down to Tunisia near the Bay of Sfax, not far from Sicily. The German's idea was to take the Suez Canal and take all the oil in Saudi Arabia. Weston's mission was to bomb those supply boats coming into North Africa.

When Weston was shot down in 1943 over the Bay of Sfax, he was bombing Rommell's troops. A French fighter got on his tail and blew him up. There had been 30 airplanes in his squadron. Weston was number three when it was over.

My brother, Weston, with my father shortly before he went overseas.

We got the details of the attack some months after it happened from a pilot who had been in Weston's squadron. After the fellow's mis-

My brother, Weston.

sions were over, he came back stateside and sold war bonds. My folks talked to him on the phone, and he told them, "If you come and see me personally, I'll tell you what happened. I can't tell you this way." Mom and Dad were living in Birmingham at the time, and the fellow was going to be at Barksdale Field, so they drove to Shreveport to talk to him. The fellow was the lead pilot for Weston. He was flying wing. He said he looked over at Weston and everything was fine, and when he looked back again, Weston's plane had been blown up.

Weston was good. He was just what you would expect for a bomber pilot who knew his days were numbered. He was going to kiss the girls hello and goodbye. Boy, he could play the horn and he was a slick marcher, but he was sure a ladies man and when they looked at him, they really gave him the once-over from head to toe.

I've got a letter that I wrote to him when he was overseas. I called him "Ugly Boy" and he called me "Bud" and we used to fight like crazy. I'm sorry that he was killed and I miss him, but he was doing what he wanted to do and he was one of jillions of boys who did. I had so many good friends who were killed as pilots.

Fort Sam Houston

Because my brother had been killed in the war, I didn't have to go overseas for my military service.

After graduating from medical school and completing my internship, I did my basic army medical training at Fort Sam Houston, close to San Antonio, Texas. It might have been titled, "*Basic* Army Medical Training," but what we had to do was to dig latrines according to specifications, distill water and do all kinds of other sanitation-type stuff.

At Fort Sam Houston, there were 400 or so fellows who had graduated from med school, had a year's internship and had gone through this six weeks' program. Out of about 400 of us, everyone was sent overseas to fight except about 30 of us who had family members who had already been killed. By the time I was assigned, Weston had already been killed in North Africa.

These 30 fellows who had lost brothers or daddies were assigned to the air base or military installation which was closest to their home towns. That's the reason I went to Shreveport. At the time I signed up for the service, Mother and Dad were moving all around, so I listed Shreveport as my permanent address because that's where my uncle was living permanently. They saw my residence was Shreveport and assigned me to Barksdale Field.

Barksdale Field

At Barksdale Field in Shreveport, my original job was as an anesthetist. While I was there, there was a Jewish doctor in the V.D. (venereal disease) ward who was just all thumbs and couldn't do a spinal tap. The colonel came to me one day and said, "Moore, I've got a problem in the V.D. ward. The doctor out there can't do spinal taps. What are we going to do?"

"I know what you're getting at," I said. "You want me to be the anesthetist in the morning and let me work in the V.D. ward in the evening."

Me at Fort Sam Houston near San Antonio, Texas.

He said, "That's right, Moore."

You see, we had to do spinal taps on all the syphilitics every six months. There were quite a few men who needed testing, and the work just wasn't being done right. Blood can test negative for syphilis, but the spinal fluid can be positive. If a person has syphilis, it affects their brain, they become neurotic and their brain deteriorates. Unless you're tested every six months, you haven't been treated properly.

Being a V.D. officer was the best job I ever had. Everyone was your friend, and they'd do anything you'd tell them to do. But they didn't talk to you if you ran into them in the officer's club. By the same token, they wouldn't squeal about me because I had something over *them*. I loved that job and I was good at it. I mean, I could do a spinal tap on someone who was out on the dance floor dancing with their partner. That's perhaps a bit of an exaggeration, but I was just really good at it because I'd done so many in Louisville.

Stealing a Christmas Tree

One funny thing I remember that happened while we were at Barksdale Field happened at Christmas time. Doris and I were married then and our son, Skip, was a year old. We needed a Christmas tree, but I didn't want to buy a tree and fool with all the decorations and stuff, so I went down to the V.D. ward where I was in charge. Over in the corner was a perfectly good Christmas tree with all the decorations, so I just grabbed it and started home with it. There I was, walking down the street, carrying that Christmas tree.

One of the guys said, "Hey, Captain! Where are you going with that tree?"

I answered, "Oh, I've got to go decorate for a party."

Thinking that it sounded like a reasonable explanation, the guy said, "Oh, OK." So I put the tree in the car and high-tailed it out of there. We still have some of those Christmas decorations from that tree!

My wife knew where the tree came from and she was mad about it, but I kept it anyway. It was all done – tinsel on it and everything – and it saved a lot of trouble and a lot of expense!

Finishing Medical Training

After I got out of the service about 1948, I went back to Louisville to complete my medical training in the general surgery residency program. I knew early on that I wanted to be a surgeon. My Uncle George was a surgeon and I'd seen people come up to him and thank him for what he had done. I hadn't particularly wanted to do anesthesia, but it was great training since I wanted to be a surgeon. I knew that if you can handle anesthesia emergencies, you can handle anything. What an education for me.

I had gotten to know a lot of the instructors at med school because I gave anesthetics for them when they came to demonstrate to med students and operate at the hospital. When I got out of the service and came back to Louisville, it was good that they knew me. There was quite a bit of competition for the surgical residency, but I was one who got the nod.

For about 18 months, I did an orthopedic residency because I knew I wanted to go to a small town and do orthopedics. With my experience giving anesthetics, I'd handled so many emergencies that nothing could come up that would flip me. I think I always had the feeling with the nurses and patients that maybe I wasn't fancy, but I could get the job done. I just worked like heck.

Here I am, standing with pride in front of my brand new Ford, the 57th car that came off the production line in Louisville after World War II. It had no radio, no heater and no air conditioner, but we thought it was great. We'd warm Skip's bottle by sticking it in the radiator opening.

Chapter Nine

Early Family Times In Canyon

After I finished my surgical training in Louisville in 1950, I started looking around for a place to practice. I remembered what my Uncle George Collett had told me, "Make sure wherever you go that there is a university or college – a school of higher learning – because it's a good place to live and you have nice people," he said. "And make sure you see Hereford cattle." That bit of advice was like a guiding principle for me.

I had a chance to go to a clinic in Louisville with 25 doctors, but I said, "What the heck? I don't want to go do that. I'll be on the faculty in Louisville, I'll be this or that, but I don't want to live in this town. Look at all the people!"

I wanted to get out where I could see Hereford cattle. I was raised to be in a small town. That's why I am here in Canyon now. When I was making my decision about where to move, I had a wife and two children. Skip had been born in 1946 and Joe had come along three years later.

For a few months, I went all over, looking for places to practice. I went to Montana because I had a friend in the service who was a surgeon in Billings and he wanted me to come out there. I went to Arkansas. I went to Indiana. I went down to Florida.

There were four different places in Texas that I considered: Longview, Ballinger, Kilgore and Canyon. There was just something about Canyon that I liked. I liked the Panhandle. I liked the plains. I liked the people. And I wasn't concerned about making money because I never made any money.

The preacher who had married Doris and me in Louisville was transferred to Canyon to become pastor of a little Presbyterian church. He went back to Louisville for summer vacation when I was still there and told me that there was a fellow in Canyon who was looking for a surgeon to come in with him.

I said, "Is there a university in Canyon?"

"Yes," he said.

"Are there cattle?"

"Yeah."

I said, "Well, I'll be out."

And that was that. In 1951, I moved to Canyon with my wife Doris and our sons, Skip and Joe. I always knew I'd do OK in Canyon. I didn't require much – just food and shelter. I figured you could only eat so much food and we only needed a small house for our small family. I liked what I saw in Canyon and I still like what I see here. I wouldn't live anyplace else.

Our "First" Kids

Our first child, *Skip*, had been born in Shreveport when I was stationed at Barksdale Field. When I found out that Doris was pregnant, I was thrilled. We named him for my father and me, giving him the respectable name of Dudley Moore, III . We nicknamed him Skip.

He was a tall, skinny, lanky baby who was born with an immune deficiency. I took one look at him and said, "Son, you just hardly got here." That poor kid was sick with allergies all the time. His nose ran constantly and he coughed all the time.

When we moved to Canyon, he had to live in a croup tent for two or three years. The tent was big enough for a single bed and it had book racks and everything in the tent. He liked to study and read. In the tent we had a radio, lights, and of course, a humidifier. He had pretty much everything he needed because he had to stay in it so much.

He didn't have any more problems after gamma globulin came out for polio and we gave him shots of it every month.

An early picture of (clockwise from upper left) Skip, Joe, Gary and Bill.

Skip always did well in music and played in the band. He grew quickly to a height of 6'4." With his athletic skills and that height, he was a good basketball player and the last time Canyon won the state basketball championship was when he played on the team.

He was always dedicated, and jumped rope four or five times every day, wearing out ropes as fast as I could buy them. Skip was always kind of a quiet kid, but he always had a sense of humor that just wouldn't quit.

After high school, Skip went to WT 1½ years on a basketball scholarship, then decided he wanted to transfer to Texas A & M. He majored in animal husbandry and range management. That's when I had the ranch down close to Bryan, Texas which I'll talk more about later. It was great for all of us because I couldn't run the ranch from Canyon and it gave Skip something to do that he enjoyed.

Joe was the next one to come along and we named him after a wonderful surgeon I had worked with in Louisville named Michael Joseph Henry. Dr. Henry sang the whole time he operated and never missed a note.

Joe's nickname was "Jaguar Joe." I don't know how Joe got the nickname, but he was always big and when he was a young boy trying to get from one room to another, he would rather go through a *wall* than through the *door*. He broke more sheetrock in the house. He was tough and he could knock things down. He was also slick as a whistle. We could have the house totally clean, then Joe could wreck it in 30 minutes or less. That was Joe.

Joe was – and is – a lot of fun and has a great sense of humor. To this day, when he calls me on the phone, we just sit and laugh which is the way he was from his earliest days. You just laughed all the time when Joe was around.

We all liked to play hard and fight. Nobody ever got killed. He was fun to be with whereas some of the others were pretty serious most of the time. All of our kids had about every type of disposition and they all ended up good.

When the boys were little, I had an electric train that I mounted on a big board so that if someone needed to sleep in the room where the train was, we could just pull the train up out of the way. It had everything: tunnels, a Santa Fe engine, stuff all around, and it was banked so you could get it going pretty fast without it spinning off the table around the corners. Joe would start that train off at full speed. When the train hit the curve, it jumped off the track, landing several feet away. When that happened, Joe just laughed. He didn't care if he wrecked the train. Joe was also musical and played in the band in high school.

After high school, Joe went to Baylor on a football scholarship and when he came home to Canyon, he brought different girls home with him almost every time. We never knew what he was going to do.

Gary, our third child, was born three years after Joe. In his younger years, he wasn't very big and, like Skip, he had a lot of allergies. Skip and Joe were pretty mean to Gary and called him the "blond headed punk." Once our fourth child, Bill, came along, the two older ones gave Gary an even harder time.

When Gary was about five or six, he finally got really fed up with his brothers and he wrote them a letter which said something like, "You folks aren't nice to me and you make fun of me and you think I can't do things, but I'll make you a promise: I'm going to grow up to do better than any of you." He signed it, "The Blond-Headed Punk."

Gary played all kinds of sports including football and baseball, but he really excelled in music and academics. He sang and always had the lead in the high school musicals, but he was a pretty good cut-up comedian, too. In Canyon, they have always had Mr. and Miss Canyon High School and Gary was Mr. Canyon. He's an extremely hard worker and always has been. He's also as dependable as heck.

Bill was the fourth child to come along and he was a pretty tough little boy. As the youngest, he was probably the most spoiled, especially by his two older brothers.

Bill was a leader and was always athletic, playing as a pitcher on the baseball team and a quarterback on the football team. He went to Baylor on a football scholarship and played football in the Cotton Bowl. When Baylor won the Southwest conference, he was on the team. As a freshman, he played quarterback but he later became the team's punter.

One funny story I remember about Bill happened in one of the televised football games when Baylor played Texas Tech. Bill punted the ball and Tech blocked it. The ball kind of spiraled up over his head, and the television cameras got a perfect shot of it happening, followed by his reaction when he said, "Oh, &^%$# !" It was the funniest thing you ever saw. Just perfect. And he never lived it down.

Grant Teaff was a very fine Baylor coach when Bill was on the team. Coaches can be very important figures to young men, and Bill still quotes him. Bill's talents weren't just on the football field or the baseball diamond because he was musical, too, and played baritone in the band. He was Mr. Canyon, too.

Northcutt's Ranch

When Skip was about 13 and Bill was about 4, one of the things we started doing together was to go to Northcutt's Ranch near Clayton, New Mexico. The Northcutts were patients of mine who had about a 15,000 - acre ranch that backed up to Rabbit Ear Mountain north of Clayton. The Northcutts and I appreciated each other, so they invited us up there whenever we could go.

It was a beautiful place, with a creek bed that ran down the valley on their ranch. The creek bed was part of the original Santa Fe Trail that went from New Mexico, up through the Oklahoma Panhandle, into Kansas and then to Missouri. The reason the creek was there was those big wagons that traveled the trail wore ruts in the land which filled with water when it rained. Eventually, there was a good-sized creek in places where the trail had been.

For about eight or ten years, the boys and I used to enjoy going up there. It was a great place to do guy things! We took our baths in the horse tank and did all that kind of stuff. We often took our own horses, but the Northcutts had extras, so we sometimes used theirs. It was a great place to take energetic young men. Though the Northcutts had their own house, they also had a guest house which is where we bunked.

One of the things we liked to do the most was have trail rides. We'd all take turns being the "trail ride master," but if Joe was the trail master, you could bet your bottom dollar you would go up or down the steepest part of the hill or into the biggest bunch of mud or the deepest creek. We'd always want to fire him, but we couldn't do it because he was so durn big.

I was always last in line if Joe was leading. One particular time I remember, Bill was on Dixie which was a nice paint we had, and Joe was leading us straight up a steep hill. I heard a loud *pop*, and here came Bill, grasping his reins, with one hand on the saddle horn. The saddle was sliding right off the horse's bottom. Joe just made us do terrible things!

One of our favorite times to go was when they were cutting and shipping the cattle. When we first started going, Bill was pretty young to get much work done, but Gary, Skip and Joe could get a lot done. I wanted my boys to know how to work because the only way they're going to exist is by doing their share of work. Over the years, they worked for a lot of farmers and ranchers around here and I tell you what, they are the best hands in the world.

The Marker in "the Thicket"

In July of 1962, we bought about 3,000 acres of land near Bryan, Texas from a fellow named Buddy Franklin. It was a pretty good sized operation with about 500 cows that Skip ran for me for awhile.

One of my favorite stories about Gary was when he was trying to find a marker in the thicket shortly after we bought the property. It was lush land, with a lot of yaupons with their long needles. When we were looking over the property, I asked the foreman, Tom Taylor, where the property line markers were. He said, "Well, there's a tree that's fallen down. It's at about a 45 degree angle. Then there's a concrete post over there. There's also one at the other end, too. We can get that one pretty easy, but I haven't seen the one further down since I was a kid. I'm not going to go down there, because the thicket is too rough."

Gary was about 10 at the time and he looked at me and said, "Pop, I'll go find it for you."

He got on his horse and started to take off and Tom said, "Man! Dr. Moore, I don't know if I would let him go down there or not. He's liable to get lost."

I said, "No, I think he'll be all right." Gary could find anything anywhere. Whenever we took a trip, he was always able to tell me which way to go. He took off down the hill and when he got down to the river bottom, he disappeared into the thicket brush.

About 30 minutes or more passed and he hadn't come back, which was longer than I thought it would take. Tom said, "Dr Moore, that boy might be in trouble down there 'cause he ought to be back by now."

I said, "Oh, we'll just give him a little more time, Tom, and see what happens."

In just a few more minutes, we saw the horse's head and then we spotted Gary. He had his arm around the horses's neck and his head flat against it. He had lost a lot of his clothes, shredded them off. When he got up close to us, Gary said, "Dad, that post is down there and that tree is there, too."

Now that's Gary.

Not too long after we'd bought the property, Skip's wife got in a car and drove off, leaving him with two little tiny babies — one in diapers and one about 2 years old. He stayed down there and was the principal and basketball coach in a little country school near the ranch.

One day he said, "Dad, I just don't want to stay down in this part of the country any more." I knew what he meant. People are different down there. Anytime you get east of I-45, the road to Houston, things get different. He said, "I want to come home." So we sold the ranch, but not before we had some really fun times there.

Tough Times

I don't want to dwell on some of the problems that our family had when the children were little, but it's important for people to understand that we had problems which we had to work through and to understand that no one's life is all good times and laughter. The tough times come and you just have to work through them the best that you can.

Doris was a fine person, but she didn't come from the most stable and loving background. Her mother's name was Agnes Greer Compton and I think her father's name was Frank Compton. He was a boilermaker for the L & N Railroad. I liked him and he wasn't a drinker. Doris's parents divorced before Doris was very old. Her father had remarried a woman who was a good, old country girl and they were as nice as they could be to me, but Doris' mother and I didn't get along very well. Unfortunately, Doris always wanted what I couldn't give her. She wanted glamour and nice things and had visions of us being big city, country club people instead of small-town, horse-loving people who lived out in the country. She became an alcoholic when we were stationed at Barksdale Field. One of our neighbors there was the wife of a medic, and they got to be drinking buddies.

Alcoholism is a disease that runs in families so it's important for my children and grandchildren to know that this has been in our family so they can take appropriate steps to prevent it. I worked in the CARE unit in Canyon for ten years and I know that there's no shame in being an alcoholic. It's a disease. The sad part comes when the alcoholic doesn't want to get well.

My uncle drove down from Crawfordsville, Indiana to see us when we moved to Canyon and he said, "Dudley, you're going to have to work awful hard the rest of your life to make this marriage work."

Things got pretty rough for our family and there were some really bad times. Doris spent six months in treatment at a hospital in White Plains, New York. When she went up there, they asked me if I wanted to stay with her or prepare her for a divorce. How's that for therapy? If I hadn't wanted to stay with her, I wouldn't have sent her up there. When we had first married, I told her that I was marrying her for life. I told her that I would never leave her, but if she ever said she wanted a divorce, we were through. She was the one who made the decision to get a divorce.

Doris

I know it was really rough on the kids and I'm sorry for that. I always tried to tell them that no matter what, their mama was a good lady and that I loved them. Anytime they asked me about their mother, I always said, "She's a good mama. She's got some problems, but you do your best."

We divorced about 1958 and I went to live with my parents who by this time had moved to Canyon to be close to us. At the time, people said, "Doesn't it make you feel funny that at your age and being a doctor in town, you're living with your parents?"

The answer I gave them was, "No, it's home to me now." Doris had a hard time taking care of the boys by herself and keeping appropriate food in the house for them, so the boys probably spent two out of three nights a week with me and their grandparents.

When Gary was about 14, he went before the judge and asked that I take custody of the kids so that's what happened. Gary caught a lot of grief for that, but he is the one who took care of his mother for the rest of her life. We all endured a lot, but we got through it.

It was good living with my parents and having the boys with us. We had breakfast together and the kids' clothes were always clean. Mom was organized. We went to church on Sunday and participated in all kinds of activities so stability and calmness returned to the household and that was good.

Chapter Ten

Our Family Expands

The boys and I rocked along in Canyon for a number of years. I lived in my parents' home with Gary and Bill. By this time, Skip and Joe had left home pretty much for good.

Eventually, our lives took another major change for the better. I had a physician friend named Virginia Willis who had trained under me in Louisville. She was living in Fort Worth and I had kept in contact with her. In 1961, Virginia called me to invite me to a New Year's Eve party that she and her husband, Theo, were going to have in Fort Worth. She said that if I wanted, she would get me a date for the party.

Even though I knew I'd have fun staying in Canyon, I decided to go to Fort Worth because it was an opportunity to go see Virginia and her friends. The date she got for me was with a beautiful woman named Lillis Thompson, who later became my wife.

Meeting Lillis

As everyone in my family knows, I'm not much of a romantic guy so our first meeting was pretty straightforward. When I got to Fort Worth, I called her and told her that I had arrived, was at the hotel dressed and ready to go to the party and just needed to know where to pick her up. Not too romantic!

She said, "Come to the grocery store parking lot. I'll be in a blue Pontiac station wagon and I'll have four children with me."

It was pouring rain, but I drove down to the parking lot and there she came. When I spotted her in the station wagon, I also saw a bunch of little noses, pressed against the windows and five pairs of eyes checking me out. At the time, it made me wonder how many other times those little noses had been pressed against the glass checking out some other guy.

Anyway, I followed her to her house and they all went in through the garage. I went up to the front door and knocked on the door. Anna Bland, who is Lillis' third child, opened the door and said, "You're not going to marry my mother!" Then she slammed the door.

I went around to the garage and went in through the kitchen. That's the way I always went in that house. I never, ever went through the front door.

Lillis and I went to the party at Virginia and Theo's and had a good time, but there was no pressure. I hadn't gone down to Fort Worth with the intention of getting married and she had a boyfriend at the time, which didn't bother me.

Courtship

Lillis was fun to be with and we always enjoyed each other's company, so our relationship was built on friendship. Her friends were real nice people and they were well-known people in the community. We became good friends who enjoyed each other.

As often as I could, I went to Fort Worth and pretty soon we settled into a schedule of me leaving Canyon every other Thursday and coming back on Sunday. Her ex-mother-in-law loved Lillis dearly and she got to be my best friend, too. One time she told Lillis, "Honey, if you don't marry that old boy, I'm going to." When we had parties, instead of Lillis doing all the work in her own home, Lillis' mother-in-law would have the party at her house and they'd have all sorts of waiters and waitresses and bellboys. It was first class.

Lillis's own mother had died at the young age of 56, but her father – we called him Poppoo – was the cutest little old devil. He enjoyed his sherry every night and always said when we poured it, "Just a little more...a little more." He had been quite an athlete when he was a young man and could tell all sorts of stories. He was just wonderful.

It was all very comfortable visiting Lillis in Fort Worth. After we'd been seeing each other awhile, I invited her to come to Canyon with a couple of friends to see the city and to meet my boys and my mom and dad. The first meeting went very well and everyone got along. When she came to visit, she didn't think it would be proper to stay at my parents' house with us. We had some real good friends named Biggen and Johnnie Duncan who were sisters and they volunteered to let Lillis stay with them. After Lillis was in town awhile, they said, "Dudley, that's the girl for you."

Anybody who meets Lillis now would think the same thing. I even took her to meet my uncle in Shreveport because I wanted her to get to know my family.

The "Proposal" and the Marriage

After Lillis and I had dated each other for a few months, I let her know that I enjoyed being with her and there would come a time when we would either decide to get married and make it a permanent affair, or if not, I'd just disappear.

One afternoon as I was driving down Highway 287 toward Fort Worth, I knew that we would be making some permanent plans when I arrived. I had reached an emotional level where I appreciated her and wanted to get married. She had been appreciative and nice to me all the time. We just needed to say *yes* or *no*.

When I got to Fort Worth and went in the back door at her house, she was grinning at me. I said, "We're going to get married aren't we?"

And she said, "Yes."

That was the proposal right there. We discussed some common sense details about children including whether she allowed this or that. As far as a romantic down-on-my-knees, "Will you marry me?" situation . . . that didn't happen. We had both reached a point in our lives where it was time to make a decision or let it go.

When we got married on April 20, 1963, we had been dating 16 months. We got married in a nice Presbyterian Church in Fort Worth in a lovely ceremony which Lillis had planned to perfection. As I remember, she wore a beautiful blue outfit and everyone looked great. The church was properly decorated and there were probably about 100 people there, all real close friends of Lillis'. My nephew, Weston, has a beautiful voice and he sang for us. My mom, dad, Uncle Will and Aunt Evelyn were all there.

Some of our friends, Cass and Jeannie Beth Edwards, hosted the reception in their home and it was great. Three or four fellows who were good friends of hers really helped me out that day when they guarded the church. We had learned that a doctor who was mad at me and jealous that I was marrying Lillis planned on crashing the wedding. I saw the guy when we were on the way to the airport, but nothing happened.

On our wedding day, April 20, 1963.

Our honeymoon was in Port Clear, Alabama which is a first class, gorgeous old-time hotel near Mobile, Alabama. We've been there four different times since the wedding. It has tradition and feeling and is the prettiest place we've ever been. There's a great big country club there with golf courses and all the finery. Inside, it was just majestic with big fireplaces and big wood structures and people all around waiting on us. They had a nice orchestra and we danced and had a real good time.

STARTING A NEW LIFE WITH A NEW FAMILY

After the honeymoon was over, we went to Fort Worth to pick up some things, then moved to Canyon. Lillis' two older children, Bea and Richard, stayed in Fort Worth to finish the school year and her two younger ones moved with us into the house on South Ridge Drive in Canyon which was the first house we lived in together.

I knew that I wanted to live in Hunsley Hills and we looked at several houses. But at the time, there were only five houses for sale in Hunsley Hills. We liked the one on South Ridge drive because it was pretty and I knew that the builder had put it together right.

When we joined our two families, everything was great. We married when Bill was in the second grade. Gary and Richard are just two months apart and they were in the 5th grade. Joe was in the 8th grade and Skip was a junior in high school. Eloise started kindergarten in Canyon and Anna Bland started first grade in Canyon. Bea and Joe are just a year apart so Bea was in 7th grade. I told Lillis, "You take care of the girls and I'll take care of boys." She agreed.

Combining our families was wonderful. Lillis had four children and I had the four boys so we immediately had a huge family. We were all *family* and I was determined to keep it that way.

I'd prepared my boys for the fact that we were going to get married and had told them that they would have a place in our house. Doris had custody of them when Lillis and I first married, but I said, "This is your home and I want you to know that even though your Mom is still living, Lillis is your mom, too because she loves you," I told them." I love her children, too. They're your sisters and brothers and we're all going to be in this game together and have a good time and mean something to each other."

Well, they kind of looked at each other and looked at me and moaned and groaned and said, "Dad, I'm hungry, do you have anything to eat?" That was about the extent of their reaction, but it worked fine.

I'll always remember when we decided to get married and got her children together. Lillis said, "What do you want them to call you?"

I said, "My children call me Pop. I want them to call me Pop." They call me Pop or Dad.

FIRST MEAL TOGETHER

The first time Lillis ever fed the whole bunch, Doris drove up just as we were getting the food on the table. We didn't know she was coming, but she dropped off all four boys and their gear. When they came inside, I said, "Hi Joe, Skip, what's happening?"

They said, "Hi, Dad! Mom is going to be gone for a while. We're just going to stay here with you all for the next four weeks."

Lillis looked kind of shocked. Fortunately, she had cooked a big meal. Skip is 6'4" and Lillis kind of shrank in comparison to him. There was a stack of fried chicken sitting up on the counter, heaped up about two feet tall.

Wherever we went, we always ate by the order of birth, with the oldest first and little Eloise last. Well, here comes Skip through the line and he eyed the great big ring of Jell-O. Skip looked at that and looked at Lillis, then took out a knife and cut that sucker in half, pushing half the Jell-O onto his plate.

When she saw what he had done, Lillis just groaned, but we just let him take it. I don't know how many handfuls of fried chicken he put on his plate, but that was our first meal with all eight kids together and I will never forget it as long as I live.

FAMILY OF TEN

Life was good in Canyon after that. We had a home. I had a lovely wife and we had lovely children and I just worked my tail off because that's what I had to do.

I'll also never forget the first time that Lillis took all those kids into church with her. She proceeded down the aisle, followed by those eight little kids. It was quite a sight!

Every time we went anywhere, we had to have two cars to carry us all. When we'd show up in a restaurant, people would say, "Are these all yours?" We all laughed about our big family.

Family times were fun times. With such an active, large family, we were obviously going in many different directions. There were times when we had boys playing football, basketball, or in the band, and girls cheerleading, twirling or doing other activities. Often, Lillis went one direction and I went another.

Coordinating everyone's schedule was quite a trick for that many people. As hard as we tried to see everyone's events, sometimes it was just impossible. Then, to make it even more complicated, I'd get a call just before I was going to leave that I was needed at the hospital. There was no choice. I had to go to the hospital. Lillis understood. We tried to find friends who were willing to take our kids places when we weren't able to. It worked.

One time when I was in Levelland or Muleshoe watching one of the kids, we lost two sets of contact lenses in one night. Eloise twirled her head real quick and the contacts popped out and Joe got hit real hard

One of our first Christmas holidays together as a family of ten. Standing left to right are Joe, Skip, Bill, Gary and Richard. In front next to me are Anna Bland, Bea, Eloise and Lillis.

and his lenses came out. We were fortunate that we didn't have too many major mishaps!

Play Hard and Work Hard

No one would ever say that I wasn't a hard worker, and I tried to instill a strong work ethic in my children. When we had 120 acres outside of Canyon, with horses and pigs and cattle, there was always lots of work to do. I always thought the boys should be the ones to get the work done.

This is how I spent my afternoon off.

We had tractors for them to ride, and if they didn't like what they were doing, I said, "Ride the &^%$# !" tractor, Boy! Get up there. I'll tell you when to quit." They all used to get mad at me, but I didn't care. I liked for them to get mad at me.

The good thing was that we played as hard as we worked. We all played sports together. We played touch football together and we cheated each other. Now that may sound kind of funny, but it was true.

Some of the best football games we had were with Dory Funk. I was their doctor and we were good friends, so we'd go out to his house out by Buffalo Lake on a Sunday afternoon. There would be Dory with his two boys, Terry and Dunk. And then there would be Rosco Richardson and his two boys. One of them played professional football and the other one was a basketball coach, and we all played together.

I played on Dory's side because I liked the way he kept score and I wanted to be on his team. If he wanted you to score, he'd say you were in bounds, but if the other team was trying to make a touchdown, he'd say, "You're out of bounds, Boy."

Of course, the only appropriate response from them was, "Yes, sir."

Dory marked the boundaries and we'd play and laugh and giggle and have more darn fun. Sometimes Cal Farley and his wife watched us. They were the ones who started Boys Ranch. They sat in rocking chairs up in their garage, just laughing at us. Cal Farley brought Dory down from Indiana to run Boys Ranch.

We all liked to play baseball and it would be the same type of thing as far as the cheating was concerned, except you did it by not counting a run.

Well, you didn't touch second base.

Yes I did.

No, I saw it.

Go on! You're out.

People would get pretty furious if they were on the opposite team, but it was all in fun.

THE GIRLS GET INTO THE SPORTS ACT

When Lillis and I married, Eloise and Bill played together all the time. She was the youngest girl and my boys made a football player out of her! When she was about five, they liked to play football in the den and pretend like they were all some of the famous football players of the day. Bill gave her the role of Roman Gabriel who was a big quarterback, and Bill was Jethro Pugh while Richard pretended to be Bob Lilly.

The boys would give her the football, then tell her to run between them and they'd tackle her.

"I don't want to be Roman Gabriel anymore," she'd say crying.

"Get back there and get this ball, " they told her and she would. It was all in fun!

Lillis and I hadn't been married all that long when we had an outside football game going and Lillis said, "I want to play."

Lillis can run like a deer, but I warned her, "Those guys might knock you down." I turned to the boys and announced that Lillis would be on their team.

They whined about it and said, "We don't want any girl on our team."

"Shut up," I said. "She's going to be on your team." Then I turned to Bill who was playing quarterback and said, "Look. Let her run down behind Joe." He was the fullback and the biggest.

Then I turned to Lillis and said, "Just get behind Joe and run as fast as you can," and she got behind big old Joe and Bill threw that ball as far as he could and she caught it for a touchdown. From then on, she was anything she wanted to be in that family.

Joe was amazed! Awed, he said, "Pop, did you see that?" We've had a lot of fun.

FAMILY VACATIONS

We took trips and had a lot of fun and of course we had the ranch down by Texas A&M. When we went down to check on the ranch, we often stayed at Hilltop Lakes in Normangee. They had golf courses, swimming pools and horseback riding. I'd enjoy being on the ranch — seeing what was going on and checking on things — while the family could be at the resort having fun.

On another vacation, we took a trip that lasted about two weeks and we never left Texas. The girls were at Mitre Peak, the Girl Scout camp down by Alpine. We drove to Midland and spent the night with some friends we have there, then drove down to Alpine to pick up the girls. From there, we drove down to San Antonio where we spent two or three days on the River Walk and all that stuff. Then we went over to Houston and spent three or four days there, going to the ball games and having all sorts of fun. After that, we headed down to Galveston where we had some good fish at Gaido's restaurant, then went on up to the ranch and stayed four or five days.

We also went to the Broadmoor in Colorado Springs a couple of times, and for almost 30 years, we've owned a house at Angel Fire, New Mexico. Originally, we had a one bedroom condo with a bunk bed upstairs, then we got a townhouse which we had about two years. After that, we bought a house with four bedrooms and three bathrooms and it's nice. It'll take care of a pretty good number of people, but now with our family being so big, it's impossible to have just one place that will sleep everyone.

Another family vacation I remember was to Durango, Colorado when we rode the train from there to Silverton. In Mesa Verde, we saw the cliff dwellings and that was something.

One of my favorite recent trips was one that I took down to south Texas with Gary, Richard, Bill and Joe. I mentioned earlier that we visited with my Kilgore band leader which was great. After that, we went over to Normangee and saw our old friends, Horace and Edna Brown, and their two daughters. Horace had been the foreman on the #2 Thicket Ranch that we owned and they still live in the house on that property.

We also got to visit with one of our special neighbors, Founty Williams, and his wife and daughter. Founty was 95 years old and we had a great time, visiting, telling stories and reminiscing about good times we spent together. It was also great making new memories with some of my boys.

We've had nice trips.

CHAPTER ELEVEN

PRACTICING MEDICINE IN A SMALL TOWN

When I first started practicing medicine in Canyon in 1951, I initially went into family practice with Dr. Bob Jarrett. He'd let me see all the new patients, or if he had patients that were going to have to wait a long time to see him, I'd see those, too.

Even though I had my all my requirements to become board-certified in surgery, you can't get your surgical boards if you do more that five percent general practice and I wanted to do general practice. I did orthopedics, I did general surgery, and I did family practice. I just did it all. I enjoyed it and I had enough training to allow me to do it well. Now there were some things that I didn't want to handle and if I wanted to ship them to Amarillo or to Dallas or Denver, that was my business. I took care of most all of it.

I had a very pleasant practice. I liked my patients and my patients liked me. I enjoyed people. I'd sit there and talk to them, asking them what they did for a living, how many kids they had, what their husbands (or wives) did for a living. I didn't just have *patients*. I had *friends* who were my *patients*.

The people who worked with me were my friends, too. My nurses, my lab technicians and my receptionist — we all had the best rapport with our patients. It was just great. There were six people working together at one time: a bookkeeper, receptionist, two nurses, a lab technician and me.

Let's Get It Done!

If I had to pick a favorite part of my practice, I'd say it was family practice because you got to know people. I got to know my patients real well and they got to know me. I enjoyed doing surgery, and I enjoyed OB. When you deliver a baby, you take care of the mother and you take care of the baby. A little bit later, the mother is pregnant again and you take care of her again and before you know it, you can go out and see babies by the hundreds that you delivered.

A typical schedule for me, if I operated, was to get to the office about 10:00 in the morning and stay until 6:00 in the evening. I tried to take an hour off for lunch when I'd go home and eat, then have a 30-minute nap, which was a life saver.

Doctors learn how to fall asleep and wake up quickly. Sometimes, I'd go to sleep on a cot down there in the hospital. Sometimes my meals consisted of peanut butter and crackers. Many times, that was my evening meal and my breakfast, too. To this day, I still eat peanut butter and crackers.

Thursday afternoons I'd take off and go out in the country and plow for a farmer. Sometimes I cut or baled hay. Other times, I combined wheat or maze. I just loved to be out on the farm.

My boys did the janitorial work at the office. They cleaned the place every night. They had to buff the floors and they had to take all the wax off every week and put new wax on. You had to have a good shine on the floor to have it look like something because you were spilling ether or chemicals on it, and getting spots on it all the time. They probably really hated me at times for making them work so hard, but that was all right.

Physician, Heal Thyself

Just a few years after I started practicing in Canyon, I came home one night with a headache and sore throat. I figured it was just something minor and thought I was going to treat myself.

That night, all the lights in the house turned yellow and my head started splitting.

We called my partner, Dr. Jarrett, then went down to the hospital for a spinal tap. I had encephalitis, otherwise known as sleeping sickness. For two months, I slept. I could hear everything that was going on and I could answer people, but I was out of it. I knew enough that I was either going to get well or I was going to die. At the time that I had encephalitis, about half of the people who got it, died. It was like polio. Since it was caused by a virus, you couldn't really take anything that would help.

I wasn't scared, but I knew enough to know that if I lived, I could be paralyzed or incapacitated in some way.

To this day, I still have no idea where I got it. None of my patients had it. The only other person in Canyon who had encephalitis the same time I did had never come to see me.

After I came out of it, I stuttered for about a year and I didn't have much feeling in my left hand and arm. I didn't do many operations for a year, but I could make a living and I could work. It really knocked me down for about two or three years.

It also changed me. When you face a potentially horrible disease like that, you have an opportunity to make some changes and I did. I appreciated living more. I decided then and there that I was going to have a little bit more humor in my life and since then, I have tried to have more fun and a better sense of humor.

A New Office – Almost

When I first came to Canyon, I had an arrangement with Dr. Jarrett to be an equal partner. After a while, I felt like I was doing more than my share of the work, but splitting the profits from the practice equally. I tried to have a discussion with him about it, but it didn't work out as well as I would have liked. So, I bought a building on the square in Canyon and hired a builder to build a new office for me. There never was any kind of "covenant not to compete" clause or anything in my contract with Dr. Jarrett.

The builders got going pretty quickly on the new building and it began to become apparent that things were happening over there. One morning, I had just delivered a baby about 7:00 in the morning and Dr.

Jarrett showed up early at the office and asked me what was going on over at the square. When I told him that it was my new office, he said, "We'd better talk pretty quick, hadn't we?"

I said, "Yes. Right now," and we did. We rewrote our partnership agreement, so I never moved. The only place I ever practiced was in the clinic in Canyon where the headquarters were later for the play, *Texas*. After our deal was settled, I paid the contractors for the work they'd already done, then sold the property to someone else. It cost me a few bucks, but it worked out better in the end.

Another smart thing we did was to have a good legal arrangement outlining what would happen in case either of us died. Two weeks after we signed the agreement, Bob died. But the arrangements were all there and his wife, Mamie, and I were friends forever.

HOME CALLS

I made a lot of home calls when I was practicing medicine. From the standpoint of a doctor/patient relationship, it was very valuable, but from the doctor's standpoint, it was a waste of time. My practice was all about doctor/patient relationships so I did home calls until my very last day.

On the last day of my medical practice, I got a call from one of my long-time patients, Mrs. Hefner. She lived to be 102 years old, but on my last visit with her, she was about 99. I'd go see her frequently when she needed me and I often took one or two of my kids with me, so they knew her real well.

Once when Bill was little and he was with me at the clinic, I got a call from her. Bill always sat in the car on my medical bag and used the handles of the bag like he was riding a horse. Then he'd carry the bag into the house for me.

My typical routine was to knock on a patient's door and just go on in, without waiting for anyone to say, "Come in." We were never very formal in Canyon.

When I saw Mrs. Hefner, I knew instantly what was wrong with her because I'd treated her for so many years. After I discussed my diagnosis with her, we had a lot of fun talking. After a while, little Bill got hungry. I said to Mrs. Hefner, "You got any food around here?"

She said, "Yes, there's some old corn bread on the stove in the kitchen." So I told Bill to go get some cornbread and he got some for all of us. After we were through eating and we'd talked enough, I said, "Mrs. Hefner, I'm going to have to leave. I've been here for what seems like an hour. Gotta get home."

She got up out of her chair, picked it up and put it right in front of the door. She said, "You're not going anywhere. You're going to sit there and talk to me because your talking means more than your medicine." And so I talked to her some more.

CLOSE CALLS

Any doctor who's honest will tell you that you can work your tail off and do the best medicine that you know how to do, but there will be accidents and close calls.

The close call I particularly remember happened after I turned my OB practice over to Bob Gross. He didn't do sections and one evening he had a pregnant woman at the hospital. He called me that night and said, "Everything's going all right, but I've got a feeling. There's something about this OB case . . . Something is wrong and I don't know what it is. Fetal heart tone is good. I just wanted to make sure you were in town."

Then, acting on his intuition, he also called the anesthetist and the inhalation therapist. I said to myself, "It's lonely there at 3:00 in the morning and he thinks he might have a problem. I guess I'd better get down there."

I put on my jumpsuit because that's the only thing I ever wore. (You can put on a one-piece jumpsuit in a hurry and be out the door as soon as you get it snapped or zipped up.) I got down there fast – right before the anesthetist and the inhalation therapist walked in.

Almost immediately, the nurse's aide said, "Dr. Gross, something happened. I can't hear the heartbeat and she's got a lot of pain in her abdomen." That aide was about 70 years old and she was absolutely invaluable for her common sense. She just *knew* something was wrong.

We went in there and Bob hollered, "Knife!" I kept a sterile knife in the operating room so if we ever needed one, we didn't have to wait for someone to track it down. It was always ready to go in an emergency.

The patient was as white as a sheet of paper. She was in shock, and didn't have a blood pressure. To take her from the bed and get her into the operating room would have taken a lot of time that we couldn't afford, so I just reached up and grabbed the sterile knife. I didn't have any gloves, I hadn't washed my hands, I didn't have scrubs on, I just made an incision right down the middle of her belly. The baby had ruptured the uterus it was up under her liver.

We got that baby out of there. It took us 2 ½ minutes from the time Bob had hollered, "Knife!" till the time I had that baby delivered. We didn't wash the belly, we didn't drape it with anything sterile. We just got the baby out of there.

The baby was in terrible shape, but the inhalation therapy man, Sappington, was great. He was as good as any big shot anywhere. He went to work on her. Eddie Garner, the anesthetist said, "She's dying. She's dying. She doesn't have any blood pressure."

I said, "Heck, I know she doesn't." I was looking at the inside of her belly which was full of blood because her uterus was split right down the middle. But to make a long story short, she lived. We worked like the devil and she lived. I still see the mother all the time and she even sent me a picture of her daughter on her graduation.

As an OB doctor, I had about four women who had ruptured uteruses. There was a big article in the paper about how rare it is for both the mother and baby to survive when that happens, but we got lucky. There was a lot of skill involved, too.

Near Miss With the Frying Pan

One night I got a call from a woman who said, "Dr. Moore, I need you to come. My husband is killing me! He's beating me up with a frying pan!" I knew her husband. He worked for the Santa Fe Railroad and I still see him and we're still friends.

I said, "That &^%$# !" is drunk, isn't he?" She told me he was. I knew she needed help. We didn't have a sheriff in Canyon. We had one police officer who covered the whole town. In fact, we didn't have an ambulance, either. The only thing we had that we could use for an ambulance was the hearse at the funeral home.

I got in my jump suit and went to the woman's house about 2:00 in the morning. When I got to the screen door, I could hear her screaming, but I knocked. When the husband heard my knock, he yelled at me. I pushed the screen door open just far enough to see that he was beating her over the head with a skillet. He spotted me right before I stepped away from the door. Just as I did, I could feel the skillet come whizzing by me. That nut threw the skillet at me, missing my head by about six inches! He looked at me and said, "Doc, I damn near got you, didn't I?"

I stopped the fight, but I'll never forget him throwing that skillet at me. For the next 30 years when he brought his wife in to the office, we laughed about my near miss. Especially him. The two of them eventually divorced and he ended up marrying two or three other women.

The Spoon Man

One of my strangest patients was a prisoner from Dimmitt who was brought into my office after he had swallowed eight spoons. He was a crazy kid who got some bread, covered the spoons with it, then swallowed the spoons.

When we took an x-ray in my office, we could clearly see the eight spoons in his belly. Fortunately, he picked spoons, instead of forks or safety pins so there were no sharp points. What were we going to do?

I said to the sheriff's officer, "Go feed him a lot of bread and bring him back tomorrow and we'll take another x-ray." We followed that procedure until he had passed all the spoons. The guards would bring a spoon in with them and hold it up saying, "He passed another one." Finally, we accounted for seven of the eight spoons.

The prisoner came in one last day for his x-ray and the sheriff's officer made a mistake. He failed to stay between the prisoner and the door. When we weren't looking, the prisoner bolted. I heard the back door bang. It was a brand new storm door and when it banged shut, it broke.

I was in another treatment room working with a little child. When I heard the crash, I figured out pretty quickly what had happened. I laid down whatever instruments I was using on the kid and said, "The &^%$# is getting away."

I took out after him and caught him on the street. The sheriff's officer was right behind me and seeing what I was about to do, he said, "Please don't hurt him." I was holding his hair, planning on jamming his head right into the concrete. I was so mad at that jerk because he tore my door up! As bad as I wanted to, I knew I shouldn't beat him up, so I stopped.

They took the fellow back to jail and I went back into the examining room where the nice little child and his mother were waiting for me with the nurse. I picked up my instruments to finish the exam and the mother said, "Doctor, you know you said a bad word, don't you?"

I said, "No, I didn't. I just chased that prisoner."

The nurse said, "Oh yes, you did."

So I got in trouble for what I'd said.

A Factor in Success is Having a Good Staff

I was always very fortunate to have a great group of people working for me who made my clinic work. They were all organized, very efficient, and never made excuses for anything that happened. They were good.

You don't make money by not paying people what they deserve and I believed in paying them well. For as long as I practiced, I always paid people better than what they could get in Amarillo or elsewhere in Canyon and I always gave excellent Christmas bonuses. I used to say to them, "You've got a good house. How did you get that?"

Their answer was, "Oh, I used the Christmas bonus you gave me." We still talk about it. *Pay people what they're worth.*

"Competition" From the North

The attitude of some of the doctors in Amarillo always struck me as kind of interesting. Many of them thought that they were the only ones

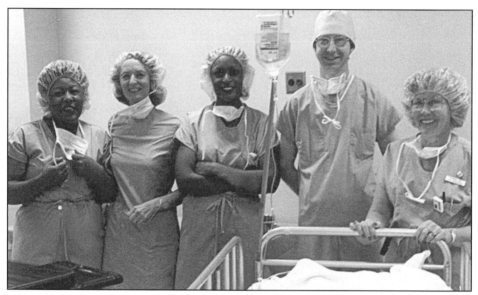

This was my first-class operating crew from left: Bobbye, Martha, Beverly, Eddie and Sandra.

who could do anything in the Panhandle. And here I was down here in Canyon doing orthopedics, general practice, surgery, and OB and they hated me in Amarillo because I was doing all those medical procedures in little old Canyon.

Some of their patients came down from Amarillo to Canyon to see me and to have me operate on them. When the doctors in Amarillo found out about it, they hit the ceiling. I said, "Look, I didn't ask them to come down to me, but they came in the front door of my office and asked me to help them and I did."

We had a lovely hospital when I first came here. It was Neblett Hospital and was where the school administrative office is now behind the square. Dr. Neblett was a practicing physician who built the hospital himself a year or two before World War II. The next hospital was Palo Duro Hospital and it closed when I retired.

Exploring the Options – and Turning them Down

I always liked practicing in Canyon and did exactly what I had always wanted to do – be a physician. I was satisfied. I was happy. I never had any regrets that I hadn't gone somewhere else to practice or done something else with my career.

Canyon couldn't have been a better place for me. The patients who came to me were good folks. They were farmers. They were hard workers. They worked for the county. Maybe they didn't even work. I had a half million dollars owed to me when I retired. It didn't make any difference. I didn't wish for anything. Maybe I'm stupid because I had chances to go to Amarillo and join clinics, but I didn't want to go to Amarillo. I still don't want to.

After I'd been practicing in Canyon about 20 years, I got an invitation to go down to the Bryan area and investigate an opportunity to practice down there. I went there with my mind open and knew what questions to ask. At the time, we had the 3,000-acre ranch near Bryan and I thought it might be interesting to explore the possibilities. Plus, I knew a lot of people in Caldwell which was about 30 miles from Bryan and was almost like my second home.

So I took the weekend off and visited the doctors around there. I sure didn't want to turn down an opportunity without knowing about it. I'll never forget the time that I was assisting one of the doctors who was doing kidney surgery. He got in trouble and I bailed him out real easy. While we were working, different doctors came in, wanting to see what I looked like.

Come to find out, those doctors down there wanted me to work *for* them. They didn't want me to work *with them*. They wanted to be the big shots and they wanted me to be the big something else.

The last doctor I went to see was a family practitioner in Bryan who laid it out loud and clear for me. He said, "We all know you're in town. The word got out that the doctor had arranged all these visits for you. I'm just going to say one thing. You'd better go home and be thankful because you will never like it here. They'll use you to death," he said.

"I know what kind of practice you have in Canyon," he added. "You are in the best place you will ever live, right where you are." He knew more about me than I did myself. I thanked him, and we sat down and visited; then I went home. He was exactly right.

THE CARE UNIT

One of the things that I worked the hardest at was being the medical director of the alcohol and drug program called CARE. I don't know if I attained much success, but I think I did. I spent a lot of time with the people in that unit, but I never spent too much time because alcohol and drug addictions are tragic conditions.

I had a lot of empathy for people who were alcoholics or drug addicts, maybe because of what I went through with Doris. In my years of practicing medicine, I had a lot of patients who had problems. For sure, I realized you don't "cure" them because they are never "cured." They can only be "in recovery." It's up to the person. If they want to quit, they can, but you can't make somebody get sober. Sometimes I challenged them by saying, "Quit kidding me, you don't want to be sober. You're a &^%$#! drunk and you're going to stay that way."

They'd give me strange looks, but it's the truth. Taking that confrontational tactic sometimes helped them face up to their problems and do something about it. One of the guys I had in the CARE unit had the worst problem I'd ever seen with drugs and alcohol, but he still calls me from time to time to tell me he's sober because he knows I care about him. "By the grace of God, I'm a sober man," he tells me when he calls. You've got to have a religious conversion and you've got to be determined that you want to be cured. If a people do those things, the good Lord will give them some more time to behave themselves.

I went overboard trying to be good to those folks and take care of them. I believe if someone gives a person a little time, that person might come around and say, "Golly, this guy really does care and maybe I'd better start caring about myself."

There were a good number of folks who recovered and the worst, the sickest, were beer drinkers because they drank so much of it. Their liver just cratered and those people got as yellow as could be. I can remember one or two whose eyeballs, skin and toenails were yellow. Their eyeballs were bulged and they were toxic, but somehow or other something good happened to them. I don't think they got the heck scared out of them. I think the good Lord talked to them one day when they looked up and asked Him for help.

A WITNESS TO HUGE CHANGES IN MEDICINE

In the 40 years that I practiced medicine, I saw huge changes. For one thing, my practice got bigger! Doing family practice, I saw 60-80 patients a day and delivered about two babies a week, a little over a hundred a year. And I did surgery between three and five times a week. I worked my tail off and I had the best workers in the world in my office.

Certainly, in surgery, there were lots of changes over the years. For one thing, we started doing laproscopic surgery for things like tubal ligations and gall bladders.

But, the three things that made the difference in medicine in my lifetime were antibiotics, cortisone and the polio vaccine. In 1940 or 1941, you had sulfa drugs, then later came penicillin which was significant because you could do operations and have something to fight infection with. Before penicillin, people might die because they had peritonitis and there was nothing to treat it with. But sulfa and penicillin made a big difference. Fortunately for me, I had antibiotics during my professional career in Canyon.

In the early days of practicing medicine, a doctor's bag contained little more than what most people had on their kitchen shelves. Some of the concoctions used before we had all the high-powered medicines that we have now were cobwebs to clot blood. You'd just take a broom and get a cobweb out of the corner, then put the webs over the bleeding. Lamp black from coal oil lamps also helped bleeding.

For bronchitis, you could use turpentine and sugar which caused the muscles in the bronchial tree to relax so the person could get some air. We also used household bleach to dress an infection and camphor oil for other ailments.

When cortisone was introduced in later years, it was a big deal. Depomedrol, a long-acting cortisone, made a tremendous difference. By the time depomedrol came out, we also had better anesthesia, better gas machines and better IV materials. Other significant drugs were cipro and erythromycin. We also had better intratracheal tubes which allowed us to give anesthetics to little newborns who needed some positive pressure.

We always had blood, we always had fluids, we always had plasma, even way back in the "old days."

Polio vaccines and other immunizations made a huge difference, too. I used to see polio cases all the time where the patient died. But, with polio vaccines, it was a different story. There hasn't been an iron lung in Canyon since 1955. I remember that because a patient of mine died of polio in 1955. You had DPT (diphtheria, whopping cough and tetanus) vaccines which made a big difference, too.

On a side note, I remember my Uncle George (who was the doctor and the person who had such a dramatic influence on my life) once said to me, "Son, a doctor makes his reputation on what he can predict will happen, not on what does happen."

For instance, in the early days, we had nothing to treat pneumonia with. The patient got well by "lysis or crisis," meaning the body broke down the pneumonia and improved or, by the ninth day, there was a crisis. If the patient didn't get better, he or she died. If the doctor could predict that a patient was going to die in nine days, he was a good doctor because his prediction was accurate.

Time to Retire

After I'd been practicing medicine for 40 years, I decided that it was time to retire. I'd seen so many changes and lived through all of them, including malpractice insurance going from $2,000 per year initially to $5,000 a month by the time I retired in 1991.

When I was about 71 years old, I remember going to John Sappington, the inhalation therapist, and saying, "John, I'm tired and when you get tired you're going to make poor decisions. I've been practicing 40 years and it's just time to quit."

He said, "I don't blame you."

Everything was going fine, but I knew the time was coming.

I still remember turning my key in the lock for the final time. I was glad. I was looking forward to it because I had everything set. I love horses and was going to have horses, which I did for many years.

On the other side of the railroad tracks from our house, I owned 10 acres that had a windmill, corral and two or three horses. After I had a bad reaction to some pain medicine recently – and the colt knocked the fool out of me – it was time to sell the horses and the property.

CHAPTER TWELVE

A Well-Rounded Life

One of the threads that has been woven throughout my life is music. Some of my earliest memories are of my mother playing the piano and all of us singing.

My mother was such a beautiful, delightful lady and she dearly loved to sing and play the piano. The old church hymns were among her favorites. I still have many of the church hymnals that she lifted from the various churches she attended. She also sang in the ladies chorus in every town that she and my father lived in. My dad, in his early days, also enjoyed singing with his rich baritone voice.

Mother, when she was about 70 years old.

I've led singing on and off through the years since I was at Baylor and made fun of the music leader that they had there. Every Wednesday for years, I led singing at the nursing home for 30 minutes. For 50 years or so, I was also the singing leader at our Rotary meeting on Tuesdays at noon.

It would be safe to say that some of the accomplishments I'm most proud of have to do with music. While I was at Kilgore High School, I

Contrary to what some people think, bass players don't just play "om-paa" music! This music was transposed for me from music originally written for the trombone. The fellow at Baylor who did it for me charged me 50¢.

played in the band with my brother and a bunch of other kids. I won first in the state in tuba, then a couple of months after that, I went on to Mississippi and won first in the south. I'd only been playing six months. Winning those medals probably made me realize that if you work hard enough for something, you're gonna get it.

My brother, Weston, was very musically talented, too and he also went to Baylor on a music scholarship. Like me, he played the tuba and like me, he won a first-place medal, but he earned his in a Louisiana contest.

Some of the medals I won for my music.

I didn't play much when I was in medical school, but I did play with a community band in Jeffersonville, Indiana about once a month. One of the doctors who worked with me at the hospital played in the band and got me involved.

When I moved to Canyon, I played with the WT band when they had some special occasion for the alumni. They always considered me an alumni because I've always been so supportive of the band since the day I came here. I've got honorary membership in all the music fraternities.

I remember trying out for the WT band with Dr. Gary Garner. When I first tried out, I made third chair out of four in the concert band. Later I graduated to the symphonic band where I've played for years.

When Gary Garner retired not long ago, we had a running joke about whether I had approached him to try out or whether he asked me.

I always enjoyed practicing my bass horn. Now, my lip gets tired after practicing 30 minutes or so, but I used to practice a couple of hours each day. Dr. Garner said if you practice an hour a day, you're keeping even. If you practice two hours a day, you're getting better!

The best band I ever played with was the West Texas A&M band in Canyon, Texas. This was taken in 1999.

THE FABULOUS FIVE

For years, one of my biggest projects has been the band scholarship fund at West Texas A&M.

When I first started helping out the scholarship fund, all they had in the endowed scholarship fund was $2,000. The director, Dr. Garner was a nice enough guy and I said, "I've got to do something to help this band. This is terrible."

Early in my life, I learned how to give. When you're a child, you learn how to tithe and give to the church. My mother tithed all her life and she made me do the same thing. Giving is part of living. You've got to pay back.

When I saw what a small amount was in the fund, and I realized that it was only yielding five or six percent, I said, "That's not going to help anybody." That's where our little band came in.

Several of us had a little band called the Fabulous Five which played for events all around the Texas Panhandle. We were having a great time at it! Then one of the band members, Raymond Raillard, and I

The members of the Fabulous Five were (standing from left) the late Creed Smith, Doug Storey, me, and the late Raymond Raillard. Seated are Garner Fielding and Billie Clinton.

decided that we could make money for a good cause AND have a lot of fun so we decided to give any money we made to the WT band scholarship fund. Pretty soon, we got the fund up to $5,000.

People said, "Golly, how did you raise that $3,000 to go in there?"

I said, "We'll we've just been playing our horns and giving you all the money."

It just kept on. When it got to $20,000, Dr. Garner just couldn't believe it. The last time I tabulated it, the total exceeded $200,000.

The most long-standing members of the band besides me were Raymond Raillard, Billie Clinton, Creed Smith, Garner Fielding and Doug Storey. (You can see, we actually had six people!)

The band has changed quite a bit since the early days, as some of our original members have died or had medical problems. We never had any problem finding people who wanted to play the old-time music with us. Sometimes, they were college students who liked the music and sometimes they were more experienced musicians.

We didn't practice. We just played. These guys were great musicians. Garner Fielding is the drummer and he was a music teacher. Can he play the drums! He plays every Saturday night at the Amarillo Club. I'm the one who organized our performances. I just looked through our repertoire and saw what would be suitable for the occasion, then I'd pick out about 15 or 20 songs.

I never told them ahead of time what we were going to play. Those guys knew how to transpose. They knew how to do everything.

Raymond Raillard. You can't believe how he could play! When he was in college, he played for dances all the time – just everywhere. During World War II, he was in Patton's outfit. He played in bands during the war, through the invasions in Europe and all the way through to Germany.

One time during the war, there was going to be a big party. Raymond was ordered to get a band together, but he had no music and no saxophone. So he started nosing around. He knew who played the piano and found a drummer who could play, and eventually the band started coming together. However, there was the "small" problem that Raymond didn't have a horn himself. He and another guy were walking down the street in some European town they had just captured and there was a little kid sitting in the gutter playing a saxophone. They just took the sax from him and gave it to Raymond. That's where he got his saxophone.

He's the only guy I've ever known who was flown from London to Paris to get some reeds to play his horn for a job that night. Raymond knew that there was a place in Paris (a music store that had good reeds) so they got him on the plane and they found the store. His stories were just phenomenal.

For 25 years, Raymond was the executive director of the play *Texas*, but he died not long ago. Creed Smith was our guitar player and he dropped dead, too. Creed joined our band one cold, snowy night in Pampa. When we walked into the place where we were going to play, Creed was sitting there with his guitar.

When I said hello to him, he asked if he could play with us. I said, "Sure!" and he played that night, then told us if we needed him again to call him and he'd come play. For the next 10 years, Creed was part of our band. Even though we usually only had five people in the band, most of us could play more than one instrument which we did when the music called for it. We had a trumpet player, a clarinet player who played saxophone, piano player, drummer, and I played the bass horn. We also had singers, but singers don't do too well at the kinds of dances we played for. We played six programs a year at the Knife and Fork club for about eight years and a singer didn't do well because everyone wanted good background music, not singing.

Some of the favorites were *Stardust, Sentimental Journey, Unforgettable,* and *Five Foot Two, Eyes of Blue*. Raymond Raillard could play *Stardust* like nobody's business. When we let the boys go on *Five Foot Two*, they just went with it! We also liked *In a Shanty In Old Shanty Town*. A good trumpet player can just take a ride on that. *Sentimental Journey* brings back memories to me, like it probably does to a lot of people.

One memory that I associate with the song was when I was in Louisville going to medical school – probably about 1941 or 1942 – and I had a date. We were on one of those paddle wheelers that goes down the

Ohio River about ten miles from Louisville. There was a great band on the paddle boat, and we danced for about three hours.

In those days, it didn't cost much to take that paddlewheel ride. Some of those boats carried big dance bands on them with 18-20 people in the band. It was pretty typical to have three trumpets, three trombones, at least five saxophones, drums, base fiddle and a guitar. That was a set for big-name bands in those days. Boy, you could just hear Guy Lombardo or Tommy Dorsey on the trombone. Ah, they were great and that boat ride was fun.

Those old songs that we played in the old days – and then in the Fabulous Five group – just transcended time. People loved to hear us play them because the songs all have a meaning to them. The older people love to hear the songs we played because that's what they were raised on. Take *I'm in the Mood for Love*. That would make you just want to smooch a girl, wouldn't it? Any girl would smooch you just to hear that song.

We also put together a quartet to sing at funerals. The name of the funeral home was LaGrone Funeral Chapel and when I was talking to the owner about a name for the group, he said, "Well, you sound like your groaning to me." So I suggested we call the quartet LaGrone Groaners and it stuck.

Mostly, we sang hymns. It's hard to say which is my favorite hymn, but you can't beat *In the Garden, Amazing Grace,* and *Just a Closer Walk with Thee*.

When we were going strong, our band of five played 85 times a year. Sometimes, we played as many as five times a week. You do that a few times and it will wear you out!

THE ROTARIAN ROAST

In 1987, the Rotary Club in Canyon began making plans to "roast" me. For several weeks, they ran advertisements in their newspaper, inviting people to submit information about anything that I did which was considered "above average" in our community.

When the time came for the official roast, it was quite a big event. Everyone involved had a great time making fun of me in every way they could think of. Of course, I did my part to make it a show, too.

REGARDING...
Dr. Dudley Moore

Dr. Moore has paid his dues and attended the Canyon Rotary Club off and on for several years. The Club feels that this ought to be worth something. We are getting desperate for news of anything he has done.

If you know of any ordinary, run-of-the-mill, usual types of things that he has done, please briefly communicate them to the Canyon Rotary Club, General Delivery, Canyon, Texas, 79015.

REGARDING...
Dr. Dudley Moore
(Sometimes known as "Terrific B." Moore)

The Canyon Rotary Club has given up on Dr. Moore. He may be the worst member we have, so he will be roasted by the Club and possibly kicked out on April 25, 1987.

If you know of any nit-wit, goofy, silly, and/or stupid things that he has done, please briefly communicate them to the Canyon Rotary Club, General Delivery, Canyon, Texas, 79015.

These two "advertisements" ran in the Rotary newspaper when they were trying to solicit something good to say about me for the Rotarian Roast.

I arrived at the "roast" in an ambulance and I was wearing a prison uniform. On the inside of my leg, I had a catheter with Budweiser beer draining into it. It looked pretty darn real.

Things got pretty crazy and I was raising heck, saying all sorts of things. At one point, Dr. Britten (who was a friend of Lillis's and mine) was invited to come up and make a psychiatric evaluation of me and he clobbered me.

One of the things that I got roasted for was that I had been in the club longer than practically anyone, but I've never been president. I said, "Well, you won't let me be. You make me lead singing."

They said that I was a terrible song leader who was always messing everybody up. Now, I think that the Rotarians sang pretty good because I'd give people heck if they didn't sing. At the Rotary meetings, it's not unusual for someone to be grinning and talking to their neighbor. If that happened, we just stopped singing and the person who was talking had to get up and sing a solo. That's one way to keep order. I don't care if they like it or not, they have to do it.

All sorts of dignitaries showed up for the roast. Grant Teaff, the former Baylor football coach, was one of them which was quite an honor since I had one son who had played football for him. Grant had a few choice things to say about me. So did Abner McCall, who was a great man and the former president at Baylor.

Someone asked Abner what kind of guy I was, and he dead panned, "I remember the name, but I don't remember him. I lived in the same house with him, too."

Paige Carruth – the former dean of men at WT and one of the best Rotarians in the Panhandle – really clobbered me, too. I just didn't have a chance.

They said some pretty tacky things about me. At one point, someone said, "We're sorry, but no one has anything good to say about Dr. Moore." They pleaded with the audience, "Is there anyone in the audience who can think of something nice?" Since no one spoke up, they all drew the "conclusion" that I had never done anything good in the 36 years I'd been in Canyon.

In reality, there were a lot of letters from people saying how I'd taken care of them, operated on them, or delivered their babies. Other people commented about how I started the Babe Ruth league in town and took care of their boys. All kidding aside, a lot of people were on my side.

It was quite an event and a lot of fun for everybody!

In Service to the Community

One of the driving forces throughout my life has been service to church and community, and I'm very proud of my work in both areas. Canyon has been good to me and it was always important for me to give something back.

In addition to my long-involvement with the band, Rotary, and singing in the nursing home, I served on the school board for nine years. For two years, I served as president. One of the perks of the "job" was to hand out diplomas at graduation. It was really special for me to be able to give diplomas to Bill, Anna Bland, and Eloise when they graduated!

I enjoyed my time on the school board. Front row, from left: Jerry LaGrone, me, and Joe Gill. Back row from left: Wesley Cox, Harold Irwin, Walter Graham and Otis Parker.

But my attempts to try to make things better wherever I lived didn't just happen when I came to Canyon. I started a lot earlier. When I was a resident at St. Joe Infirmary in Louisville, some of the guys would say, "Gosh, I wish we had a basketball team here so we could play in these city leagues."

I said, "Let's just do it."

Their response was, "Well, I don't have time."

But, I believe that you always have time for what you want to do .

I went into the doctor's lounge when everyone came in to change clothes before surgery, and I "requested" donations to get the basketball team started. I raised $350 and in 1945, that was enough money to buy the uniforms and everything. It seemed like I had money coming out of my ears. When the sister superior found out how much money we raised, she also arranged to install some big, portable basketball goals in the auditorium.

If you set a goal, you just have to go after it and get it done.

Years later in Canyon, I helped raise more than $3,000 for polio at a basketball game between the Rotary Club and the WT faculty. We Rotarians dressed like girls and the faculty dressed in long winter underwear.

We started out asking people to put their donations in the small cups we passed around, but had to alter our approach after a little girl with braces on her legs walked out onto the middle of the basketball court. Then, the cups literally overflowed. When that happened, we asked everyone to just throw their donations onto the gym floor where we very quickly swept them up.

I'm proud of my involvement with the Babe Ruth baseball league which I started in Canyon and the baseball parks that I helped build. I was president for 11 or 12 years, so I was really committed to it! But, it was a family affair. If the ballpark needed mowing, I'd get my kids out with about three mowing machines and we could mow the whole world in an hour. We had a regular army.

Another big milestone for me was when I was honored at "Dudley Moore Night" in March of 2003. More than 300 people showed up for dinner, music and entertainment in a special, fun-filled evening on the WT campus.

The WTAMU Foundation and the Friends of Fine Arts planned the event as a tribute to me for the time, effort and money that I've contributed to the fine arts department of the college and the Panhandle. Now, they didn't have to do that, but I really appreciated it. The things that I was honored for that night were things I did because I wanted to, not because anyone pushed me.

The funds that our Fabulous Five band have raised now represent the largest single source of scholarship aid for WT band students. Some of the kids who get those band scholarships might not be able to go to college if it weren't for the scholarships.

I loved seeing my family and friends there and hearing the things that were said about me, which were mostly nice and all in fun. It was great to hear the Fabulous Five band play before the festivities started, then hear the PEP band, which is made up of students and faculty members. They played the WT school song, which you would have expected. But, the band also played the fight songs from my alma maters, Baylor University and even Kilgore High School. It was probably the first time that the Baylor fight song had ever been played on the WT campus!

I've been active in the WT foundation for many years, and served as president for two years. Our whole purpose was to provide financial support for the university. We also helped by recruiting and providing good will.

Before that, I was on the Baylor University Foundation Board where I served for 15 years. For three years, I served as president of the Baylor Parents' League. We often went down to Waco for football games and the Pigskin review.

I guess you can say that community service has been a part of my life for a long, long time. It's important to serve your community!

Chapter Thirteen

Reflections

There comes a time in every person's life to take stock of what you have, reflect on the past and look toward the future. Here are a few of my thoughts on a variety of subjects.

Never A Ladies Man

I know that this personal history might be read by some of my grandchildren one day, so I want to be sure and point out a few things. . . some serious and some not so serious!

For one thing, I was never a ladies man, but I did have a girlfriend from time to time. Kids always think these things are interesting so I'll tell a couple of stories just to give my grandkids another perspective on their grandfather.

When I was in medical school in Louisville, I was engaged to a girl I knew at Baylor named Evelyn who was a wonderful person. I had an apartment in Louisville which I had started furnishing for our forthcoming marriage. She lived in Dallas, and one day she called me out of the blue and told me that she didn't want to get married.

I said, "I know you're honest about it and I'm glad you called me, but I'm sorry about this," and we broke up. The reason I think she broke up with me is that she and my mother didn't get along.

When I was an intern a couple of years after she broke the engagement, I was walking down the hall at St. Joe's Infirmary when they told me that I had a call. It was Evelyn and she said, "Dudley, would you take me back so we can get married?" I had to tell her that I was already engaged to another woman. When we had the Baylor 60th reunion, I saw her again.

Memories of My Parents

When my parents moved to Canyon, it was the best move they ever made. For me, it was a wonderful opportunity to get to know them in an entirely different way.

My dad was a good man who was severely wounded by the Depression. I was a young boy during the Depression and he and I didn't speak for a whole year even though we were living together in the same house. He just couldn't stand me doing anything better than Weston because my brother was *his boy*. I was *Mother's boy*.

When I won First Place in the South for playing a horn, he never said anything, but it didn't bother me. My mother was congratulatory. I knew my dad had been hurt because of the Depression, and I was sensitive to that. It bothered my mother that Dad wouldn't talk to me, but she accepted it. Besides, I had my stupid brother to fight with any time I wanted to so we were in good shape.

My brother, Weston, who had died during World War II, also had a son named Weston. When my brother died, Mother and Dad took responsibility for raising their grandson. After Mother and Dad moved to Canyon with the young Weston in about 1956, Dad was finally in an environment which he should have been in all his life. Instead of being around steel mill workers and factory workers and construction workers, his friends were the president of the university, professors, and intellectually just a higher class of people. He joined Rotary like me and that led to many friendships.

When they came to Canyon, we were living about a mile and a half out in the country on 120 acres with two houses. Our family lived in one house and Mother and Dad lived in the other. Having been originally a farm boy, Dad loved country living. We had a barn and he had fun adding on to it and making all sorts of changes. One thing Dad really enjoyed was taking care of the 4,500 hens that we raised. He and Mother collected the eggs and sold them at Taylor and Sons to people who would raise them into beautiful Arbor Acre White Rock hens.

Dad could do just about anything. Electrical man that he was, he could fix anything. If the Rotary needed a float built for a parade, he could do that, too. Once we moved into town, Dad walked quite a bit, but he didn't like to walk on the sidewalk because it was uneven (or there was gravel). He walked with another man right down the middle of the street.

My dad, George Dudley Moore.

Dad should have been one of two things. He should have stayed in the army – he was a captain when he left – or he should have been a college professor. My dad was a Bible teacher you wouldn't believe and a very academic man. He read all the time and could quote scripture to you, but he didn't often do it in the course of a conversation. I can still see Dad sitting in his chair reading with those green visors that the railroad workers wore to keep sun out of their eyes. He thoroughly enjoyed living in Canyon. At the time, I was a member of First Baptist Church, and they joined the church as well. Dad taught a men's Sunday school class.

He wasn't a big man, probably only about 5'10" or so and he weighed about 145 pounds. In his early days, he had dark hair, but then he lost his hair like I did, but not as much as I did.

When he got older, Dad had little strokes for about two or three years. He'd get better for while, then he'd have another one. After one of these strokes, he'd kind of sleep all day for two or three days. When he announced that he wanted some ice cream, we would know that he was getting better.

Mother spoiled the heck out of him and always got up and made his coffee. One morning, she asked him if he wanted a cup and he said "yes" like he always did. She went into the kitchen to make it, and when she took it to him, he was dead. He had a massive stroke, and just died right there which was a great way to go. He died April 28, 1970 at the age of 83. It was Lillis' birthday.

My mother was a beautiful woman. She only went to school through the eighth grade, but you would have thought she had a PhD. I don't know why she never had more school than that, but she was worked as a stenographer for years. She could play the piano beautifully and she was a lady, just like Lillis. When we were growing up and poor, she did a beautiful job sewing clothes for my brother and me. She even made outfits out of the sacks that feed used to come in.

After she came to Canyon, she flitted around and got involved in everything. Just like in every town she'd ever lived, she started singing and playing the piano for the junior high school kids. Even

Mother on her 90th birthday with Lillis' Aunt Ruth and our granddaughter, Allison.

when she was 90 years old, she played the piano every day and sang songs.

One of the most memorable songs for our family was *The Little Ship Was On the Sea*. Mother used to sing the song to me when I was a little boy and continued the tradition with my grandchildren, Gary Paul and Trudy. When they came to Canyon to take Mother out to lunch, she'd often sing the song to them. It had special meaning to Mother because the men in her family were all captains on the Great Lakes, and it also had spiritual significance.

The Little Ship was On the Sea

The little ship was on the sea
It was a pretty sight.
It sailed along so pleasantly
And all was calm and bright...
It sailed along so pleasantly
And all was calm and bright.

When low and behold a storm assailed.
The wind blew loud and long.
It blew the ship across the sea
And rolled the waves along...
It blew the ship across the sea
And rolled the waves along.

"Master we perish, Master we fail!"
They cried; the master heard.
He rose, rebuked the winds and waves
And stilled them with a word...
He rose, rebuked the winds and waves
And stilled them with a word.

Mother and Lillis were the closest of friends. I think it was partially because Mother reminded Lillis a little of her own mother. The two of them would go shopping, eat lunch out and do just everything. Lillis just thoroughly enjoyed my mother.

Up until the last five years of her life, Mother was very healthy. She drove a car until she was 92. I can still see my mother driving to Amarillo to shop and have a good time with three old fuddy duddies in the car with her. Here she was, 90-something years old.

When we told my mother she couldn't drive anymore, she just said, "OK," and put the car into the garage. Three or four times a week, she got into it and backed it out of the garage. Then she'd take a mop and wipe the dust off the car.

Mother died September 9, 1996 at the age of 102. The night she died she said, "Dudley, you be a good boy." What did she expect me to be? I was 70 years old, but she still thought of me as her little boy.

In the front of a hymnal, we found this list that Bea had written of things that reminded her of her grandmother, my mother:

Home-made custard always in the refrigerator. (Mother always made egg custard that she put into little glass dishes. When the kids came into the kitchen, they'd run to the refrigerator for one of those fresh, delicious treats.)
Home-made cookies. (Usually star cookies, or sugar cookies with a cherry in the middle)
Playing hymns on the piano (*Somewhere My Love* from the movie, Dr. Zhivago, was one of her favorite melodies.)
Old toys in the bottom drawer. (In the bottom drawer of a roll-top desk were toys the kids liked to play with. It also held Lincoln logs which she used to build a village – complete with lights and cotton for snow – at Christmas)
Always dressed up including matching beads, earrings or pins
Doll and buggy in the closet
Stories about her mother from England, about her father, about the Depression and hard times

Let's Get It Done!

<u>Grandma</u>

1. Home-made egg custard always in the refrigerator
2. Homemade cookies:
3. Playing hymns on the piano & "Somewhere my Love" from Dr. Zchalgo
4. Old toys in the bottom draw — Lincoln logs, pick-up-sticks, cowboy & Indian guns, plastic army men
5. Always dressed up — including matching ~~bead~~ beads & earrings or pin
6. Doll & buggy in the closet
7. Stories —
    about her mother — from Eng.
    about " father —
    about the <u>depression</u> & hard times

Lessons Learned

During my 85 years of experiences, I've learned a lot about life. One of the things I've learned is that you don't *make* your children do anything. In all my years of practicing medicine, I saw a lot of parents trying to make their children be something they weren't. It just doesn't work.

Sometimes people ask me if I'm disappointed that none of my kids wanted to become a doctor. The answer is no. They saw me stay up all night, answer the phone at 3:00 in the morning, then get up and go to the office or the hospital early in the morning. At one time or another, all my kids have said, "Pop, you'd come home for awhile, then go right back to work. You worked all the time." That's my fault that I couldn't turn down patients who needed me.

I was with my kids as much as I could possibly be. We had a phone at the baseball diamond for me to call my patients. If somebody wanted me, the sheriff would come by, or the phone would ring at the park, and I'd answer it. If all I needed to do was call the druggist and order a prescription, that's what I'd do. If my kids were playing ball, I never left the park unless I absolutely had to.

Greatest Accomplishments

Certainly my greatest accomplishment of all is having such a wonderful family. I have had good children and a great home life once I got married to Lillis, who is a first-class lady. My family has always been the type of family anyone would have wanted... We had a lot of fun. We all worked. My children did what I told them to or else they got in trouble. When they were growing up, I always believed in spanking them if they needed it. Even when I was on the school board, I thought that the teachers needed to be able to whip the kids. I still believe it.

We had fun. We played together. We ate together. We cheated each other. We just had a good time. I was with them as much as I could possibly be. When we had the half-section farm by Dawn, we plowed and planted. We were always working because I believed it was important to work and that it was important to keep kids busy and stimulated. But, you have to be good to them, too.

We haven't had any major heartaches or tragedies and the kids have all been good. Even good families have problems and we were fortunate that nobody ended up getting shot or stole anything or any of that junk. It's all been good.

Now, I'm not going to say that it was perfect, but when there were problems, we worked them out right away. If the kids fought with each other – like all kids do – they either worked it out or I helped them work it out when I got home.

After Lillis and I were married, my kids knew we loved them and her kids knew we loved them. There wasn't enough money in the world for all that bunch, but they all got a college education. Skip, Gary and Richard went to A&M. Anna Bland, Joe and Bill went to Baylor. Eloise went to Texas Tech and Bea went to SMU. They're all doing OK and I'm proud of every one of them.

Another great accomplishment was having a family that managed to survive during the Depression. To coin an old expression, we'd *root hog and die.* This is an expression from the old days which means if you're going to succeed, you'd better get on with it.

We tried to do everything we could just to keep going, and were lucky to have a good family backing us that included not just moms and dads and brothers and sisters, but aunts and uncles, too. The Depression made me realize that some people just have to work real hard to survive. We worked hard and we *survived*.

Going down to Baylor and getting a scholarship was a big thing for me because that enabled me to go to a good college. Once you get your foot in the door, you can make it from there on. Whatever you want to do, you've always got to try hard to get your foot in the door.

Just getting accepted to medical school was a pretty good accomplishment because in those days a lot of guys didn't get accepted, just the same as today.

Getting a score board for Canyon was a good accomplishment. When I first came here, they were griping about needing a score board at the college stadium. I asked, "Why don't you have one?"

"We don't have it appropriated," they said.

My response was, "Appropriation, heck! Let's get it!" So I raised $500 and we got the score board and it stayed forever.

Guiding Principles

One of my greatest attributes has always been that *if I have a job to do, I do it*. The job comes first. No hocus pocus. No excuses. Nothing would take its place. If I'm supposed to be somewhere at 5:30 in the morning, I'm there at 5:30. That's the way I was in my practice. Anytime there was something that needed to be done, I was there to get it done. I say, if something needs to be done, do it. Start it and do it.

By my nature, I have always been aggressive. Just like when I won my first contest on the bass horn. I would have smacked that guy if he had beaten me! I've always worked hard – like when I was working on the boats – and I'm not afraid to work extra hours. I don't care what you're going to pay me. If you've got a job, let's get it done.

I demanded of my nurses that *patient care was the first priority* and we all worked hard for our patients. I'd say, "Don't you sit around there talking if somebody is out there needing help. You get out there and help them." That's the reason we could see so many people in a day. Everybody worked and we were cross-trained in every job.

Cleanliness is important. In my practice, everyone knew things had to be clean. Boy, I tell you I couldn't stand dirt. I still can't. Things have to be clean.

Respect for the flag is important. When I was working on the Babe Ruth League, I made them always raise the flag and stand at attention while the national anthem was played. That's what we did for every single game as long as I was there. Now, they don't do that as much. I believe you've got to have that stuff.

Friends are important. We have enjoyed many friendships throughout the years. I don't need a lot of friends, but the friends I have are good ones. I never really tried to cultivate friendships because we had such a big family and I figured that I didn't need to be hugging and kissing strangers. As it has turned out, Dr. Cornett and all the college presidents have been real good friends of mine. It just happened.

Work is a pleasure. I've worked real hard throughout my life and I expect my family to do the same. I believe that work is a pleasure and some people don't realize that. One of my pet peeves is people who don't carry their load, because I always did. Ask me why I went down to the office on Saturday morning. People needed me! I'd work six days a week because people needed me. If I didn't want to hire out, I shouldn't have been a doctor.

Donating and Tithing

If you're not raised giving money, you never will. That's where tithing when you're a child comes in. My mother always had us tithe and that's the way my life has been. She made us pay a nickel out of every 50¢ that we got. I don't need all my money. I guess it would be nice to have it, but I have had enough money ever since I started practicing. So I give it to the church. I tithe. It says to tithe. Don't argue with it. Do it. Shut up.

Church

From the time I was a very small child, church has always been very important to my family and me. Whenever the church doors were open, we were there and that's something I've tried to instill in my children.

Though I was raised Baptist and went to Baptist churches all my life, I'm a member now of the First Methodist Church in Canyon. Making the transition from being a Baptist to a Methodist happened when Lillis and I were getting married. We were consulting with Lillis's pastor in Fort Worth who was a Presbyterian and a very fine man. When we brought up the fact that I went to the Baptist church and she went to the Presbyterian church, he said, "They're both fine, but why don't you just go to a neutral church?"

I said, "Fine. We'll go to the Methodist Church," and we've been there almost 40 years.

I'll never forget the time that we went to church here shortly after we were married and Lillis walked in with all our eight children parading behind her. It was quite a sight!

When it came time to build a new church, I was the financial chairman of the building committee and we were proud to raise all the money we did. I sang in a choir for 35 or 40 years. I've hit a lot of bad notes, but I can fake it real good.

Advice

My children and grandchildren have already heard all the advice that I have offered to them through the years. Probably, more than they would have liked! But, if I had another opportunity for them to pay attention to some more of my "words of wisdom," here is what I would say:

Always plan an alternative route. When young men or women are planning their lives, they may have certain expectations of what's going to happen. For instance, a person may plan to get married and live happily ever after. Maybe that will happen and maybe it won't. Maybe the marriage won't last, so you'd better have some alternative in mind. No matter what, I'd prepare myself for a profession and I would make it a tough one so that everybody can't get into it. Do something that not everybody can do.

The other advice I'd give is: *Work hard at whatever you do.*
Be polite and go to church.
That's it in a nutshell.

Illnesses and Operations

Up until the past few years, I've been very blessed with good health. One of the first operations I remember is when my uncle George Collett took out my appendix in Indiana on Christmas day. It made me mad because I missed Christmas dinner.

When we lived in Alabama, I had my tonsils taken out. My dad carried me to the doctor on his back and carried me home. I recovered in the waiting room where all the patients waited.

I got an inguinal hernia working at the ranch. I like to say that I got it because my son didn't hold up his end of a railroad tie. I remember hearing it "pop."

In recent years, about every two years, I've had some kind of surgery including back surgeries, neck surgery and surgery for prostate cancer. That's enough cutting, I can tell you.

My latest episode happened when I went in to have a pain treatment and had an allergic reaction to the injection the doctor gave to me which was supposed to alleviate my persistent back pain.

The injection didn't hurt. But afterwards, the doctor told me to move my legs so I could get off the table I was lying on. I told him I couldn't move.

He said, "You're not breathing good, are you?"

I said, "No, I'm not."

I knew what was happening. Whatever medicine he gave me was going up the spinal cord and causing a reaction so that I got numb from the belly button down, then from the xyphoid process to the top of my rib cage. As I felt the numbness creeping over me, I said, "Boy, I'm in trouble." I knew if it went much higher, it would go to my brain and that's too much. I couldn't move my arms. I couldn't move my legs. Then, I passed out.

I learned later that they gave me oxygen, then blood pressure medicine to get my blood pressure up. An ambulance came and the guys put me on the stretcher.

Here poor Lillis was listening to all of it through the wall. God knows what went through her mind, but I was passed out and couldn't move. I had an anaphylactic reaction to the medication. I don't know what they gave me. It was seven or eight hours before I got feeling back and in the months since it happened, my recovery has been steady, but slow.

Life In General

I really have enjoyed life. I guess it's because I'm not looking for bad things. I enjoy where I'm living. You can take me out and sit me out in the middle of the prairie there and some guy from New York might say, "Man, how do you get *out* of here?"

And I'd say, "Just sit down. This is pretty good, fella." That's the way I look at it.

I've had a fine family. Lillis is a great wife and is the best thing that ever happened to me. How lucky can you be? It's all luck. A lot of it is. You can figure it out the best you want, but you're not gonna win them all. I got a wonderful wife.

I would hope that people accept me for what I am and what I've done. If I haven't done enough, sorry. That's the best I could do.

I've attained everything that I think is important. Now, I didn't say that I *wanted*. But I haven't wanted for a lot because I never had a lot when I was a kid. Just give me an old mouth piece at home and I'll blow it.

All I need are the little things. I always had a garden at home and I had chickens. Just little things. That's all I need. That's all I need now.

I've pretty well supported the community. It's not worse off because I'm here. It's a little better off. That's about the best you can do.

Strolling near the dock in Nice, France.

These two pictures depict my life . . . the goats, barn, and horses in the top picture with my Suburban filled with horse feed and my bass horn in the bottom picture.

I didn't make as much money as I could have made, but I made enough. I was just busy treating people. If you couldn't pay me, so be it. Most of my patients paid me, but if they didn't, I still wave at them if I see them on the street. No hard feelings. I know how it is not to be able to pay a doctor's bill. There was times that my mom and dad couldn't pay a doctor's bill. Everyone is supposed to do some charity work.

Some people might say in response to that, "Well you didn't expect to do enough. You didn't try to make $4 or $5 million a year like some doctors do."

My answer would be, "No, I didn't try to do that." That's not my disposition. I came to a small town and I was a small town doctor and I saw my Hereford cattle and a university, just like my uncle advised me to do. And we're very fortunate with raising children and you can't beat that.

We've traveled all over. We've been to New York four or five times, going from there to the entrance of the St. Lawrence and on into Nova Scotia and Quebec. We've been all over the Caribbean, the Mediterranean and through the Panama Canal. We've been to England and France. We went on the *Mississippi Queen* from New Orleans to Vicksburg. We've been to Alaska. We've been lots of other places. We've been. We've been. What do you want to see? I sure don't want to see Afghanistan. I don't want to go anywhere. I want to stay home.

If something happens that things aren't going to be so good and physically I'm not going to be good, that's all right. After 85 years, I've seen a few football games. I've had a good run at it. I really have.

I don't expect a lot and that's OK. In Kilgore, we lived in a two-room shack and that was good enough for me. Our whole house there wasn't as big as what I have for a kitchen now. We had coal oil lanterns and pumped our water. It was enough.

As Good As It Gets

There are moments in everyone's life when they say, "This is just the best there is . . . this is the greatest." For me, that moment comes in the evening when I'm sitting on my back porch, looking out over the

Our house in Canyon, Texas at 178 T Anchor View, where we have lived since 1991.

A family gathering on Christmas day in 1977. Standing from left are Wink, Bill, Dema, Joe, Lillis, me, Paula, Gary, Skip and Richard. In front from left are Anna Bland, Bea with Allison, Eloise, Dannielle, Ty, Pappoo and Mom.

countryside. I don't need to have a beer or a glass of whiskey. A glass of cool water is just fine.

Now, that's living. Sometimes our dog, Candy, barks at the jackrabbits like she's the boss of the place. But, she won't catch anything. She sits there and looks around while I count the cars on the trains that go by. It's great.

Where can you sit in the clean air with the flag flying and people going by and trains going by and see as far as you can see? Man, that's living.

LOVE FOR THE FAMILY

As I'm reflecting about a lot of things, I want my family to know that I love them. I do. Everything I've ever done has been for my family. I worked my tail off. I went through that miserable divorce, but I've never run their mother down to the boys. I never will. And Lillis' children have been the sweetest children and Lillis has been the greatest wife. I've been loved by my kids and I love them. But I expect them to do right and do the best they can.

That's all I ask.

My view from our back yard.

Pops
by Allison Clark House

There was a caring man of curative arts,
He studied for years the anatomy and knew its parts.

In Birmingham, Alabama he was born,
And for 70 years he played his tuba horn

Because of years of stress upon his back
A picture perfect posture did he lack.

In stature, this humble man was rather tall
But with eight children, his family was not small.

Thick locks upon his head, they were not there,
In fact, his shiny head was rather bare.

Sardines and onions were always his favorite treat,
And never a total stranger did he meet.

His jovial sense of humor was never lacking
The jokes he told he never did stop cracking.

Self-discipline to his children he did preach,
And setting a goal in life he did teach.

His speed in driving his car was always slow,
And singing in the choir, his voice was low.

A doctor's coat he always wore by day,
But overalls would be his choice, he'd say.

His idea of being relaxed was feeding his horses.
So he kept a barn and let nature take its courses.

As a healing man, his patients he put first,
And many a night a sick one he did nurse.

Surgery was the specialty he did love,
He depended upon guidance from above.

After 40 years of practice did he retire
But his love for people will always be on fire.

The man I have described, I know so well,
He's my POP I'm so glad to tell!

Crippen family, clockwise from back: David, Eloise and Leah.

Gary Moore family, clockwise from upper left: Trudy, Gary Paul, Paula and Gary.

Bill Moore family, clockwise from upper left: Elaine, Josh McCloud, Bill and Will.

Joe Moore family, clockwise from upper left: Dema, Joe, Julibeth and Jody.

Thompson family, clockwise from upper left: Angel, Richard, Angela and Paige.

Aston family, clockwise from back left: Anna Bland, Scott, Mary Kate and AnnaLee.

Skip Moore family from left: Jamie, Brooke, Skip, Chrisa, Ty and Dannielle.

Clockwise from upper left: Wade, Curtis & Allison House, Eloise, Bea and Wink Clark.

Hopes for the Future

I hope my kids continue having good families and they will. They have just the greatest children and I want them to be good parents and do the best that they can in the business world.

We all have different capabilities and I know it. It doesn't make any difference to me who makes the money. I just want them to be happy in what they're doing. However you define success, some will have more of it than others.

We've had some tough times and there will be more in the future, but it's important to support each other. It's a good world, but it's not easy all the time.

What Matters Most

There's no question. What matters most is family. That's it.

A Final Note

Not long ago, a mother asked me to write down some words of wisdom for her son who was becoming an Eagle Scout. Here is what I wrote:

Love the Lord

Set goals – high goals. You don't want to do something that everybody can do.

Be a leader. There are a lot of followers in the world.

Keep music in your life

Keep a sense of humor

That about sums it up.

Lillis and me.